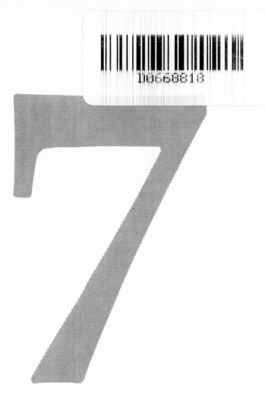

Unauthorized *Harry Potter Book 7* **News**

W. Frederick Zimmerman, NIMBLE BOOKS LLC

Nimble Books LLC

ISBN: 0-9765406-0-6

Copyright 2005 Nimble Books LLC

Last saved **2006-05-10**.

Nimble Books, LLC
2006 Medford Suite C127
Ann Arbor, MI 48104-4963
http://www.nimblebooks.com

Table of Contents

Nimble Books LLC

Book description

Through the magic of electronic publishing, this "nimble" guide to the work of best-selling author J. K. Rowling provides the latest news about Harry Potter book 7, updated whenever there are significant developments. The first major element of the book is a detailed, chapter-by-chapter analysis of *Harry Potter and the Half-Blood Prince*. Unlike a conventional book, for which editions are printed in quantity every couple of years, this "living book" goes through frequent "mini-editions" and is printed fresh whenever customers place an order. **Purchasers are entitled to free PDF updates, forever.** See below for details.

This version was most recently updated May 10, 2006. An entirely new section of analysis with **more than 80 new pages** was added in October 2005; a section of trademark analysis and title predictions was added in December 2005; and April 2006 saw some much-needed proof-reading.

This book replaces *Unauthorized Half-Blood Prince Update* (ISBN 0975447939), which is now out of print. ✗

Publisher's Comments

SOURCES

The reporting and analysis in this book is unofficial, unauthorized, and unconfirmed.

LAYOUT

You may notice that major sections or mini-chapters usually begin on a new page, which often results in the preceding page being rather short. This is deliberate, partly for stylistic reasons, and partly so as to allow frequent updating as new information is released about Harry Potter Book 7.

HOW TO GET FREE PDF UPDATES OF THIS BOOK

Proof of purchase of this book (in either paperback or e-book format) entitles you to free PDF updates, forever!

We accept proof of purchase in two (2) formats:

- E-mail receipt from your on-line retailer forwarded to HP7-updates@nimblebooks.com.

- Photocopy of receipt sent by mail to Nimble Books LLC, 2006 Medford C127, Ann Arbor, MI 48104-4963. Don't forget to include your e-mail address!

Tip: Don't bother asking your retailer for a free update! They won't know what you are talking about and aren't set up to help you. You must contact Nimble Books directly via updates@nimblebooks.com.

Notification of PDF updates is delivered to you via e-mail.

Unfortunately, we can't offer the free update in paperback form, since it costs us money to print and ship each copy.

For those who are curious about how often we update, the answer is that it is determined by the intersection of the occurrence of significant news and the sensible management of costs. Our electronic printer, Lightning Source, charges us fees every time we update the source file for a book. So we try to be strategic about when we do updates–but we love taking advantage of technology to deliver a superior product! ✔

Author's comments

READ THIS BOOK IF ...

- You, or someone you love, have enjoyed J. K. Rowling's Harry Potter books.

- You want to learn interesting things you may have missed in the Harry Potter books.

- You like challenges. I'm going to try to keep things clear for you, but I'm also going to teach you how to learn about subjects that interest you – and that means reading challenging stuff, just like Harry, Hermione, and Ron have to do at Hogwarts!

DON'T BOTHER IF ...

- You are totally uninterested in children, young adults, or fantasy fiction. (In other words, if you are a complete and hopeless Muggle!)

SPOILER WARNING: STOP HERE IF ...

- You don't want to encounter spoilers.

A "spoiler" is advance information about a book or movie that would "spoil" the experience of seeing the actual work. Book and movie reviewers generally take care to warn readers of potential spoilers. Internet posters who have advance information that others may not yet have seen usually include the word "SPOILER" in the title of their article, and sometimes add extra lines to their post or otherwise hide their content so that casual readers have additional protection against encountering spoilers.

> This entire book should be considered to have a SPOILER warning affixed. If you really hate getting advance info about books or movies, don't read this book!

Having done my duty and issued a spoiler warning, I can now tell you that there are no *true* spoilers in this book: there are no secrets revealed that would ruin any dramatic surprises in Harry Potter Book Seven. Instead, there is a patient, searching accumulation of many details found in the public record. Put together, these details will add much to your understanding and appreciation of the "Harry Potter" series.

Warning: I have no sources of inside information and I have not spoken with or heard from J. K. Rowling, her publishers, her film company, or anyone who is in any way officially connected with the books. The contents of this report are unofficial and unauthorized. Although J. K. Rowling, etc. have not confirmed any of the specific statements in the book, I have taken great care to tell you where I found particular pieces of information. When the source is J. K. Rowling, you can probably count on it! Otherwise, it's speculative.

UNDERSTAND HOW THIS BOOK IS ORGANIZED AND WHAT IT CONTAINS

This book is loosely grouped into four major parts:

- Analysis of *Harry Potter and the Half-Blood Prince*.

- What is known about Harry Potter Book Seven.

- Information on books by Rowling *beyond* book seven.

- Appendices.

As research for this book, I read:

- Every on-line chat that J. K. Rowling has ever done.

- More than 500 news articles mentioning the quoted phrase "Half-Blood Prince" in a leading news warehouse and more than 475 articles identified by Google News as mentioning the quoted phrase "Half-Blood Prince."

- More than 500 blogs mentioning the quoted phrase "Half-Blood Prince" in the blog search engine Feedster.

- More than 2000 articles posted on Usenet newsgroup alt.fan.harry-potter.

- Hundreds of posts on dozens of Potter-related websites.

- Dozens of trademark applications at the UK and US patent offices.

- Numerous biographies and critical works about J. K. Rowling.

- And, of course, the entire series to date!

This book contains the results of my research. Over the years and especially with the publication of *Harry Potter and the Half-Blood Prince*, J. K. Rowling and others have let slip quite a bit of information about the series. I think I was able to pull together a lot of interesting ideas. You will notice that there are many quotations and that wherever possible I have provided an "attribution"—that is, I have identified author, title, date, and place of publication (often Internet). That way, you can judge for yourself whether my sources are solid. ✎

Author bio

ABOUT THE AUTHOR

W. Frederick Zimmerman is the publisher of Nimble Books LLC. He earned a B.A. with Honors from Swarthmore College and a J.D. from Wayne State University. He has read all of the Harry Potter books with his daughter Kelsey. He read the first three to her aloud, before she got too smart for him. He lives in Ann Arbor, Michigan, USA with his beautiful wife Cheryl and their children Kelsey and Parker.

ABOUT NIMBLE BOOKS

Our trusty Merriam-Webster Collegiate Dictionary defines "nimble" as follows:

```
1: quick and light in motion: AGILE  *nimble fingers*

2 a: marked by quick, alert, clever conception,
comprehension, or resourcefulness  *a nimble mind*  b:
RESPONSIVE, SENSITIVE  *a nimble listener*
```

And traces the etymology to the 14th Century:

```
Middle English nimel, from Old English numol holding much,
from niman to take; akin to Old High German neman to take,
Greek nemein to distribute, manage, nomos pasture, nomos usage,
custom, law
```

The etymology is reminiscent of the old Biblical adage, "to whom much is given, much is expected" (Luke 12:48). Nimble Books seeks to honor that Christian principle by combining the spirit of *nimbleness* with the Biblical concept of *abundance:* we deliver what you need to know about a subject in a quick, resourceful, and sensitive manner.

ACKNOWLEDGEMENTS

First, last, and always, my lovely wife, Cheryl.

Our wonderful daughter Kelsey.

Our wonderful son Parker, who may just grow up to be a Harry Potter fan.

Harry Potter fans everywhere, who shared so much useful information with each other and with me.

Jeff Guillaume.

Dave Haber.

The great folks on alt.fan.harry-potter, including Troels, Ard Rhi, zgirnius, Jim McCauley, Karnak17, Kish, Louis Epstein, Richard Eney, and Blon Fel Fotch Passameer-Day Slitheen.

And, of course, J. K. Rowling, for giving the world these books that reflect love, intelligence, generosity and courage. ✗

Editorial reviews

Here are some of the positive reviews for my previous J. K. Rowling, Unauthorized Half-Blood Prince Update, also published by Nimble Books:

"The Unauthorized Half-Blood Prince Update," by W. Frederick Zimmerman is a must for any Harry Potter fan who has enough time to read this website. (http://www.TheBoyThatLived.net)

I loved the information in the "Unofficial 'Half-Blood Prince' Update", because I am a Harry Potter fan, and me and my kids will be in that bookstore at 12:01am on whatever day the next volumes emerge, but I was even more interested in the methodology used to sift and assess all those random bits of information (lost sheep?) roaming the internet. This is a pathfinder for a fundamentally new kind of book, and I would be interested in seeing the same methodology applied elsewhere. And as an added bonus the author's prose is both lively and concise, making this a very pleasurable book to read. (Greg S. Davidson, Amazon.com review, http://www.amazon.com/exec/obidos/tg/detail/-/0975447939/104-3812520-0008711?v=glance&ref=ed_oe_p&st=*)

The author of this book …is taking advantage of "Print On Demand" technology to update the book whenever new information has been released. It has already been updated at least once since September 30. This is an excellent example of the merits of Print On Demand technology in that it allows the author to make sure that the book never becomes outdated. Kudos to the author for not only providing a very well written book full of interesting and pertinent information, but also for using new technologies that allows his readers to keep up to date. (Mimi Cummins, http://www.hpbook6.com)

Want to know who the Half-Blood Prince is? Want to know what the last word of the last Harry Potter book will be? A new book called "The Unauthorized Half-Blood Prince Update", by W. Frederick Zimmerman, pulls together everything fans know so far about the next Harry Potter book, and beyond. …In more than 100 info-filled pages, the new Half-Blood Prince Update book very clearly lays out everything we know about the book so far, following all the fan rumors and speculation, debunking the rumors we know to be false, and documented with interviews J.K. Rowling has given on the subject.

A fan of the books himself, Mr. Zimmerman read all the Harry Potter books with his young daughter Kelsey, reading them aloud to her until, he says, she got too smart for him after the third book. His book is very heavily documented with quotes, so you know exactly who said these things and when they were said, making this book an important source of information you'll want to refer to over and over again. (Dave Haber, Executive Editor, Wizard News, http://www.wizardnews.com/story.200411023.html) ⚡

How to pronounce "Rowling"

Stephen Fry is an English actor who is the narrator of the Harry Potter audio books. In an interview in 2003 he cleared up a crucial issue.

> Stephen Fry: Can we settle a really important question? How do you pronounce your last name?

> JK Rowling: It is Rowling - as in rolling pin.

> Stephen Fry: Rolling! You now all have to say after me, the word "rolling" boys and girls, 1...2...3...

> Audience: ROLLING!

> Stephen Fry: If you hear anybody in the future say JK "Rowelling" you have my permission to hit them on the head - not with a copy of the Order of the Phoenix because that would be cruel

> JK Rowling: That would kill them :o)

> Stephen Fry: No use something smaller than the last book—like a fridge. JK Rowling (laughs) (MSN UK, 6/26/03, http://www.msn.co.uk/liveevents/harrypotter/transcript/Default.asp?Ath=F)

BUT YOU CAN CALL HER "KEVIN"

In December 2004, Rowling put to rest another misconception about her name.

> According to a recent article in a UK newspaper, I am known to my good friends as 'Joanie'. Just for the record, nobody, in the whole course of my life, has ever called me 'Joanie.'

> I'm looking forward to finding out what my husband calls me. 'Kevin," perhaps. (jkrowling.com, http://www.jkrowling.com/textonly/rubbishbin_view.cfm?id=5) ✗

Christianity and Harry Potter

The Harry Potter phenomenon has sparked a great deal of controversy among Christians. Obviously, my own view is that the Potter books are good for children; but as a Christian, I feel a responsibility to acknowledge and address the issues before encouraging readers to plunge into this book.

THE FUNDAMENTAL ISSUES

One fundamental problem is that the Bible is full of very clear commands forbidding the practice of witchcraft, while the Harry Potter books are full of elaborate descriptions of witchcraft and wizardry. See, for example, Deuteronomy 18:10:

> Let no one be found among you who sacrifices his son or daughter in [or who makes his son or daughter pass through] the fire, who practices divination or sorcery, interprets omens, engages in witchcraft … [NIV]

Another fundamental problem is that the Bible is full of very clear commands that members of the Body of Christ should spend their time on loving Christ and following the Bible, whereas the Bible is not at all full of commands that we should spend our time reading children's books and novels.

ROWLING'S OWN VIEWS

J. K. Rowling has been close-mouthed about her own religious faith. Here is the most candid personal statement I was able to find.

> **E:** But in your own life, I mean, are you a churchgoer?
>
> **JK:** (Nods) Mmm hmm. Well I go more than to weddings and christenings. Yes, I do.
>
> **E:** And in your own life, would the church and that kind of spirituality help you deal with the loss of your mum?
>
> **JK:** No, actually it didn't at the time. No. (Shakes her head)
>
> **E:** So you've come back to it.
>
> **JK:** Yeah, I would say so. I have some problems with conventional organized religion. Some problems. (Long pause) But…but, yes, it's a place I would go to in a time of trouble. It probably is a place I would go to in a time of trouble. I wouldn't expect it to provide all the answers, 'cause I would expect to find some of those within me.

> **E:** Right, but the institutional side of it, you know, the rules…
>
> **JK:** I have certain problems with some aspects of that. Yes I do. (CBC Hot Type interview, 7/13/00, http://www.cbc.ca/hottype/season99-00/00-06-23_interview.html)

I might mention here that quite a few important Christians, such as Martin Luther, John Wesley, and, hey, *just about every other Protestant alive since 1519,* have some problems with certain aspects of organized religion.

In the spirit of fairness, it is clear that J. K. Rowling may have some Christian sympathies and feelings, but she is not a practicing, committed, believing Christian. The question is, does that mean we should shut the door on her books?

WHAT I BELIEVE

It seems clear to me, having read all her books and every published interview that I could find, that J. K. Rowling does not intend for children to throw themselves into the practice of witchcraft.

It also seems clear to me that Christ did not intend that Christians should only enjoy works of art produced by practicing Christians.

The word Christians use is "discernment." We must be careful to discern the true meaning and true implications of what we read. With that in mind, here's my bottom line.

I believe that J. K. Rowling's agenda is to tell a cracking good story that encourages children to make good choices. When you read, remember that this is a pretend story, and remember that the Bible tells us to be very careful about witchcraft and wizardry, and focus on what J. K. Rowling is trying to tell us about goodness and love.

As the Gospels say,

> "where your treasure is, there your heart will be also." (NIV, Matthew 6:21, Luke 12:34).

So put your energy into the aspects of J. K. Rowling's story that are highly compatible with Christianity. Jesus told us:

> 'Love the Lord your God with all your heart and with all your soul and with all your mind. This is the first and greatest commandment. And the second is like it: 'Love your neighbor as yourself.' (NIV, Matthew 22:37-39).

When you read J. K. Rowling's books, let it be for the glory of God. ✁

Possible Titles for
Harry Potter Book 7

We searched the trademark databases at the United Kingdom's Patent Office
http://www.patent.gov.uk/tm/dbase/ and the United States Patent and
Trademark Office http://tess2.uspto.gov/bin/gate.exe?f=tess&state=q8m5sh.1.1
for trademarked titles beginning with the words "Harry Potter."

U.K. Trademark Search results 12/10/2005

Mark Text	Date	Status
HARRY POTTER	09.09.1998	Registered
HARRY POTTER	02.09.1999	Registered
HARRY POTTER	14.12.1999	Registered
Harry Potter	07.06.2000	Registered
HARRY POTTER	19.08.1999	Registered
Harry Potter	06.06.2000	Registered
HARRY POTTER AND THE ALCHEMIST'S CELL	26.04.2000	Registered
HARRY POTTER AND THE CHAMBER OF SECRETS	22.10.2003	Registered
HARRY POTTER AND THE CHARIOTS OF LIGHT	26.04.2000	Registered
HARRY POTTER AND THE GOBLET OF FIRE	28.06.2000	Registered

HARRY POTTER AND THE GOBLET OF FIRE	22.10.2003	Registered
HARRY POTTER AND THE GOBLET OF FIRE	26.04.2000	Registered
HARRY POTTER AND THE HALF-BLOOD PRINCE	24.07.2003	Registered
HARRY POTTER AND THE ORDER OF THE PHOENIX	04.04.2003	Registered
HARRY POTTER AND THE ORDER OF THE PHOENIX	26.10.2000	Registered
HARRY POTTER AND THE PRISONER OF AZKABAN	22.04.2003	Registered
HARRY POTTER AND THE PRISONER OF AZKABAN	22.10.2003	Registered
HARRY POTTER AND THE PRISONER OF AZKABAN	22.04.2003	Registered
HARRY POTTER AND THE PYRAMIDS OF FURMAT	26.04.2000	Registered
HARRY POTTER.COM	26.06.2000	Registered
HARRY POTTER.COM	26.06.2000	Registered
HARRY POTTER AND THE BATTLE FOR HOGWARTS	24.07.2003	Withdrawn
HARRY POTTER AND THE CURSE OF THE DEMEN+	09.06.2004	Withdrawn
HARRY POTTER AND THE DEATH'S HEAD PLOT	09.06.2004	Withdrawn
HARRY POTTER AND THE FINAL REVELATION	24.07.2003	Withdrawn
HARRY POTTER AND THE GREAT REVELATION	24.07.2003	Withdrawn
HARRY POTTER AND THE GREEN FLAME TORCH	24.07.2003	Withdrawn

HARRY POTTER AND THE HALLOWS OF HOGWARTS	24.07.2003	Withdrawn
HARRY POTTER AND THE HOGSMEADE TOMB	24.07.2003	Withdrawn
HARRY POTTER AND THE HOGWARTS HALLOWS	24.07.2003	Withdrawn
HARRY POTTER AND THE MUDBLOOD REVOLT	24.07.2003	Withdrawn
HARRY POTTER AND THE PARSELTONGUE TROPHY	24.07.2003	Withdrawn
HARRY POTTER AND THE QUEST OF THE CENTAUR	24.07.2003	Withdrawn
HARRY POTTER AND THE REALM OF THE LION	24.07.2003	Withdrawn
HARRY POTTER AND THE SERPENT PRINCE	09.06.2004	Withdrawn
HARRY POTTER AND THE SERPENT'S REVENGE	24.07.2003	Withdrawn
HARRY POTTER AND THE SHADOW OF THE SERP+	24.07.2003	Withdrawn
HARRY POTTER AND THE TOWER OF SHADOWS	09.06.2004	Withdrawn

The SpongeBob connection: All the trademark applications listed above were filed by a company called "Seabottom Productions Ltd."

U.S. Trademark search results:

HARRY POTTER AND THE ORDER OF THE PHOENIX	LIVE
HARRY POTTER AND THE ORDER OF THE PHOENIX	LIVE
HARRY POTTER AND THE ORDER OF THE PHOENIX	LIVE
HARRY POTTER AND THE ORDER OF THE PHOENIX	LIVE
HARRY POTTER AND THE ORDER OF THE PHOENIX	LIVE
HARRY POTTER AND THE HALF BLOOD PRINCE	LIVE

HARRY POTTER AND THE HALF BLOOD PRINCE	LIVE
HARRY POTTER AND THE HALF BLOOD PRINCE	LIVE
HARRY POTTER AND THE HALF BLOOD PRINCE	LIVE
HARRY POTTER AND THE HALF BLOOD PRINCE	LIVE
HARRY POTTER AND THE SERPENT PRINCE	LIVE
HARRY POTTER AND THE SERPENT PRINCE	LIVE
HARRY POTTER AND THE SERPENT PRINCE	LIVE
HARRY POTTER AND THE SERPENT PRINCE	LIVE
HARRY POTTER AND THE CURSE OF THE DEMENTOR	LIVE
HARRY POTTER AND THE CURSE OF THE DEMENTOR	LIVE
HARRY POTTER AND THE CURSE OF THE DEMENTOR	LIVE
HARRY POTTER AND THE CURSE OF THE DEMENTOR	LIVE
HARRY POTTER AND THE TOWER OF SHADOWS	LIVE
HARRY POTTER AND THE TOWER OF SHADOWS	LIVE
HARRY POTTER AND THE TOWER OF SHADOWS	LIVE
HARRY POTTER AND THE TOWER OF SHADOWS	LIVE
HARRY POTTER AND THE DEATH'S HEAD PLOT	LIVE
HARRY POTTER AND THE DEATH'S HEAD PLOT	LIVE
HARRY POTTER AND THE DEATH'S HEAD PLOT	LIVE
HARRY POTTER AND THE DEATH'S HEAD PLOT	LIVE
HARRY POTTER AND THE GOBLET OF FIRE	LIVE
HARRY POTTER AND THE GOBLET OF FIRE	LIVE
HARRY POTTER AND THE GOBLET OF FIRE	LIVE
HARRY POTTER AND THE GOBLET OF FIRE	LIVE
HARRY POTTER AND THE GOBLET OF FIRE	LIVE
HARRY POTTER AND THE SORCERER'S STONE	LIVE
HARRY POTTER AND THE PRISONER OF AZKABAN	LIVE
HARRY POTTER AND THE PRISONER OF AZKABAN	LIVE
HARRY POTTER AND THE PRISONER OF AZKABAN	LIVE
HARRY POTTER AND THE PRISONER OF AZKABAN	LIVE
HARRY POTTER AND THE PRISONER OF AZKABAN	LIVE
HARRY POTTER AND THE CHAMBER OF SECRETS	LIVE
HARRY POTTER AND THE CHAMBER OF SECRETS	LIVE

HARRY POTTER AND THE CHAMBER OF SECRETS	LIVE
HARRY POTTER	LIVE
HARRY POTTER	LIVE
HARRY POTTER	LIVE
HARRY POTTER	LIVE
HARRY POTTER	LIVE
HARRY POTTER	LIVE
HARRY POTTER	LIVE
HARRY POTTER	LIVE
HARRY POTTER	LIVE
HARRY POTTER	LIVE
HARRY POTTER	LIVE
HARRY POTTER	LIVE
HARRY POTTER	LIVE
HARRY POTTER	LIVE
HARRY POTTER	LIVE
HARRY POTTER	LIVE
HARRY POTTER AND THE SERPENT'S REVENGE	DEAD
HARRY POTTER AND THE SHADOW OF THE SERPENT	DEAD
HARRY POTTER AND THE REALM OF THE LION	DEAD
HARRY POTTER AND THE QUEST OF THE CENTAUR	DEAD
HARRY POTTER AND THE MUDBLOOD REVOLT	DEAD
HARRY POTTER AND THE HOGWARTS HALLOWS	DEAD
HARRY POTTER AND THE BATTLE FOR HOGWARTS	DEAD
HARRY POTTER AND THE HALF-BLOOD PRINCE	DEAD
HARRY POTTER AND THE HALLOWS OF HOGWARTS	DEAD
HARRY POTTER AND THE HOGSMEADE TOMB	DEAD
HARRY POTTER AND THE SHADOW OF THE SERPENT	DEAD

Leaving out the titles already used in the series, and the titles withdrawn in the U.K., this leaves us with four titles that are alive in the U.S. only:

```
Harry Potter and the Death's Head Plot
Harry Potter and the Curse of the Dementors
Harry Potter and the Tower of Shadows
Harry Potter and the Serpent Prince
```

And three titles that are alive in both jurisdictions:

```
Harry Potter and the Alchemist's Cell
Harry Potter and the Chariots of Light
Harry Potter and the Pyramids of Furmat
```

Since Rowling is a U. K. author, the titles alive in the U. K. would seem to be most likely. Let's take a close look at each possibility.

Harry Potter and the Alchemist's Cell

What does this bring to mind? Alchemy … Nicholas Flamel … the philosopher's stone … methods of prolonging life … Voldemort … Horcruxes …

Alchemy … potions … Snape … Harry's mother Lily. As we will see in the chapter-by-chapter analysis below, J. K. Rowling goes to a lot of trouble in book six to establish that Harry's mother Lily was a skilled potioneer, *and* to bring Harry up to speed on potions via Snape's book. Hmm.

Yes, we could be in the right ballpark here. Does the title tell us anything else about the story?

Well, there are a lot of different kinds of cells that come to mind:

- Prison cells
- The cells in a honeycomb
- A cell in a conspiracy
- Cell phones

Any of these might make sense, although I have to admit I would be very surprised if the resolution of the Harry Potter series hinged on Lily Potter's cell phone.

Harry Potter and the Chariots of Light

What about this one? Chariots … Rome … "Gladiator" … Russell Crowe … oops, wrong turn!

Let's try that again … Chariots … horses … centaurs?

Light … vision … goodness ….

Now we're getting somewhere!

As I discuss in the chapter-by-chapter analysis below, it really seemed to me that Rowling went out of her way in book 6 to emphasize that both Trelawney and Firenze (aka "Dobbin") are still at Hogwarts.

The centaurs are noble, good creatures; they have excellent vision; they are magical, they are neutral, they are headquartered near Hogwarts (which is the favorite place of both Tom Riddle and Harry Potter) … one could easily imagine the centaurs playing a key role in Harry Potter 7.

Although it is perhaps a stretch to imagine them pulling chariots … that seems unlike their prideful nature.

Harry Potter and the Pyramids of Furmat

Frankly, if *Pyramids of Furmat* is the title, I'll eat my hat.

I just don't see much likelihood that after six books where he never leaves England, Harry Potter would wind up in magical Egypt for book 7.

It seems very likely to me that the most important characteristic of the word "Furmat" is that it is highly trademarkable, because it is a coined word with no prior meanings.

I think this one is a red herring, pure and simple.

When will we find out the real title of book 7?

Don't expect to find out the real title until well after the release of "Harry Potter and the Half-Blood Prince." At the Edinburgh Book Fair in August 2004, Rowling was asked about the title of book 7, and said:

```
"I'm not going to tell you, I'm sorry. The trouble I would be
in if I did. My agent would have me hunted down." (Sunday
Times,8/20/04)
```

This *is* a bit of a puzzler. She's the *autho*r, after all.. Why *can't* she reveal the title?

My best guess is that the publishers and movie companies are concerned about protecting their intellectual property. There would be an immediate rush to hijack domain names and trademarks. So Rowling is under pressure to make sure everyone else has time to do their jobs properly.

Chapter-by-Chapter Analysis

Chapter 1 The Other Minister

SMART-ALEC SUMMARY: The Muggle Prime Minister meets his current counterpart, Cornelius Fudge, and Fudge's successor, Rufus Scrimgeour, and gets caught up on what's been going on in the Wizarding world.

POINTS TO PONDER: It bothered me that the Muggle Prime Minister is shown as rather a silly buffer. Wouldn't it have been a bit more plausible for him to be a little tougher-minded? Or, for that matter, for *her* to be more of a Margaret Thatcher type.

Some Internet posters thought I was worrying about nothing. "Juvenal" wrote:

> "That's broadly how I envisaged the scene before this book: the PM being let into the secret in a Yes, Minister style. JKR's lightly satirical portrayal of a generic PM is similar to other portrayals of politicians in recent British literature and programmes that aren't directly political, and fairly unexceptionable. "

This triggered a great thread in which "Kilroy[1]" offered up a terrific "Yes, Minister"/Potterverse cross-over parody. (For background on "Yes, Minister", see the Wikipedia entry[2].)

> Imagine what Sir Humphrey Appleby would have to say about it.
>
> PM: Humphrey, I've just had a visit with a most extraordinary man.
>
> SH: Really, Prime Minister? Who would that be?
>
> PM: It was strange, he was dressed very oddly, wearing a cloak and a bowler hat. He came into my office through the fireplace. He called himself the Minister for Magic.
>
> SH: Oh, you mean Fudge. Yes, I wasn't expecting his visit until at least tomorrow. I would have thought he would have given you at least a day to get acclimated before he made his visit.
>
> PM: You mean to say..
>
> SH: That there really is a Ministry for Magic? Why yes of course, Prime Minister. They manage the affairs of all the wizards and witches in Britain. You know, keep their world separated and hidden from ours. I would have thought Fudge would have mentioned all of this to you.

---

[1]Chad S. Dansby, Denton, Texas, is an educator, philosopher, renaissance man, humanitarian, and all-around good guy. His favorite flavor of Bertie Bott's Every Flavor Beans is varnish.

[2] http://en.wikipedia.org/wiki/Yes%2C_Minister

PM: Well, yes. He did, but I thought it was some mad joke. You mean to say there are real witches and wizards living in Britain, that can do real magic?

SH: Yes, of course Prime Minister. I'm with the Civil Service. We know everything.

PM: And how long have you known about this, Humphrey?

SH: Oh, well I personally have know about this since I became the Cabinet Secretary, but several of the senior Civil Servants have known about them for years.

PM: For years? And the Civil Service has covered this up?

SH: This was not a cover up...it was responsible discretion exercised in the national interest to prevent unnecessary disclosure of eminently justifiable procedures in which untimely revelation would severely impair public confidence.

PM: But how many of these magical people are there?

SH: Well, Prime Minister, we really have no idea. The people at the Ministry for Magic have done an excellent job of keeping their world hidden from us.

PM: But surely, we should do something to find out just how many of them there are.

SH: Well, Prime Minister, your administration is still in its first months and there is an awful lot of other things to get on with.

PM: Humphrey I know there are other things to get on with, but I think we need to have legislation that will keep track of all these magic people.

SH: Well of course, Prime Minister, something certainly ought to be done, but is this the right way to achieve it?

PM: Yes, Humphrey, I do think this is the right way to achieve it.

SH: Prime Minister, this is, simply, not the time, for all sorts of reasons.

PM: What sorts of reason could there be? This is a democracy, Humphrey. The people have a right to know what its government knows.

SH: No, Prime Minister, the people have a right to be ignorant. Knowledge only means complicity and guilt. Ignorance has a certain dignity. Besides, what would Her Majesty's Loyal Opposition think if you, only a few days into your term as PM, were to suddenly announce to the nation that there are real wizards and witches? You would be out of office by the end of the week.

PM: Yes, Humphrey, I think you're right. I think we can put this legislation on the back burner for a while. No need concern ourselves with witches and wizards. Besides, there is a certain dignity in ignorance.

```
SH: Yes, I thought you would see it that way.³
```

POINTS TO PONDER: I loved the passing reference to the magic painting in the Muggle Minister's office. It triggered some fun thoughts. As far as I can recall, there's never been a reference to a spell that lets "real" people enter the painting world.

Wouldn't that be cool? Another method of near-instantaneous transport. I wonder if Voldemort will go after the painting network in book seven ... it would be a tremendous way of consolidating his power. I can imagine Harry or, more likely, Hermione, finding the right spell (*"two-dimensionalicus"?*) to get into the painting network. That would be a great sequence.

Arguments against this idea: apparently the security on the existing network is extremely effective, otherwise they wouldn't have paintings in Dumbledore's office or the Muggle Prime Minister's. As Fudge comments at the end of the chapter, "the other side can do magic too."

Louis Epstein had some interesting follow-up ideas:

> I suppose if ghosts can be petrified, paintings can be too...Voldemort might do that.
>
> I don't see it being used for travel as opposed to communication...but of course portraits of Grindelwald or Slytherin might be feeding information to Death Eaters... and I wonder if a "good" painting could be submitted to the Imperius Curse?

And Troels Forchhammer commented:

> The ability of the portraits to affect the real world seems severely limited. They can speak and watch, but very little else (unless their canvas happens to be in a place where some extra magic has been added; as for instance the entrance to the Gryffindor Tower at Hogwarts).
>
> The ability of the portraits to move between paintings seems passing strange to me -- apparently they can move from painting to painting in the same building, but between buildings only between their own portraits.

(Excellent observation!)

> I somehow doubt that any of the other portraits (for instance Sir Cadogan) can get into the paintings in the Headmaster's office, and since there would only be the one magical portrait in the office in 10 Downing Street, only that one wizard can enter it.

---

³ http://tinyurl.com/b8get

POINTS TO PONDER: On close reading, there does not appear to be any direct reference to the person later revealed to be the "half-blood prince" in this first chapter.

POINTS TO PONDER: It struck me that JKR was curiously emphatic about having Fudge revisit the list of calamities in the Muggle world with the Prime Minister. Unfortunately, no giant clues leaped out at any of the readers I talked with. Troels had the most plausible explanation (albeit not especially dramatic) drawing on a previously published interview with JKR:

> JKR: I'm going to tell you as much as I told someone earlier who asked me. You know Owen who won the [UK television] competition to interview me? He asked about Grindelwald [pronounced "Grindelvald" HMM…]. He said, "Is it coincidence that he died in 1945," and I said no. It amuses me to make allusions to things that were happening in the Muggle world, so my feeling would be that while there's a global Muggle war going on, there's also a global wizarding war going on.[4]

Troels wrote:

> This is, IMHO, more of that same thing -- the result of the separation between the Muggle and Wizard communities not being complete.

WHY I LOVE JKR: This is the chapter where we meet Rufus Scrimgeour and realize that JKR put a massive head-fake on us with the August 2004 release of this snippet of text describing Scrimgeour.

> He looked rather like an old lion. There were streaks of grey in his mane of tawny hair and his bushy eyebrows; he had keen yellowish eyes behind a pair of wire-rimmed spectacles and a certain rangy, loping grace even though he walked with a slight limp. (jkrowling.com, 8/20/2004).

Wow, sounds like a great character, eh? Unfortunately, the reader of chapter 1 swiftly realizes that this guy has absolutely nothing to do with "the Half-Blood Prince." You've got to admire JKR's proficiency at getting her fans "off their feet" (as in, the end result of a head fake in basketball). All we can do is watch as she motors past us to the goal.

UNFORGETTABLE MOMENTS: To tell the truth, there really aren't any unforgettable moments in this first chapter. If all the chapters in the book were this pedestrian, this would be a jolly, good-humored novel of no enormous distinction: "fluff."

---

[4] http://www.the-leaky-cauldron.org/extras/aa-jointerview3.html

Chapter 2 Spinner's End

SMART-ALEC SUMMARY: Two Goth witches pay a visit to Severus Snape's slimy living quarters and extract a surprising promise from him.

POINTS TO PONDER: When Narcissa asks Snape to step in and perform the deed if it seems Draco will fail ... that's not much to protect Draco, is it? If Draco gets to the point of probably failing, he's also at the point of probably being in a lot of trouble with Dumbledore.

Karnak17 pointed out:

> I think that if Snape is determined to protect somebody, then that is quite a bit of protection.

This is absolutely right! I significantly underestimated Snape's prowess as a wizard right from the beginning of *HBP*. Now that I look back at it after all the discussion and the work that went into this book, I realize that in some sense the *whole point* of *HBP* is that Snape is an extremely good wizard. After all, he's the title character!

POINTS TO PONDER: The Unbreakable Vow sure sounds effective, and, as we know, Snape eventually fulfils it--but was it really? Only JKR knows if there might be a way of releasing someone from an unbreakable vow.

POINTS TO PONDER: There's very little discussion of Snape's living quarters ... just why is he temporarily here in a Muggle neighborhood? Is that what he prefers (because he's a half-blood?) or is there more to it?

Again, Karnak17 was more insightful than I.

> I got the impression that it was Snape's permanent home, where he returns every summer. I assumed it was the house where he grew up.
>
> I liked the description of the sitting-room as a padded cell. I think Rowling is trying to indicate that Snape turns everyplace where he stays into a sort of dungeon or prison -- as he does with his DADA classroom later in the book.
>
> If the house is his father's, it also would be a way of pointing out that even though his past is ugly, he is trapped there. He can't move beyond it. Which is a recurring theme in these books. (Like with Sirius in Grimmaud Place.)

POINTS TO PONDER: There's what is Peter Pettigrew up to? He usually has a sneaky angle of his own ... what is it here? The most obvious explanation is the one given in the text, that Voldemort set him there to watch over Snape.

One poster thought Pettigrew was too much of a "witless germ" to have any secret agenda:

> I can't really agree with that assessment -- Peter is
> generally a witless germ seeking the protection of those
> stronger than him. The only bit of actual independent thought
> he has shown was to manage to get to Voldemort and help him.

Subsequent readers made the noteworthy point that Pettigrew was a significantly better wizard than the senior members of the "Gang of Four" (James, Remus, and Sirius) thought him—and they are all quite accomplished wizards as teens and as adults. I guess it will be in book seven that we will find out just how good a wizard Peter Pettigrew is ... and whether Voldemort's silver hand gives him any extra edge!

POINTS TO PONDER: It's emphasized how astounded Bellatrix is... exactly *why* is she so astonished?

Karnak17 cleared it up for me with this very nice point:

> She thought he was a traitor loyal to DD. By promising to
> kill DUMBLEDORE or die trying, Snape has -- from Bella's point
> of view -- PROVED her suspicions incorrect.
>
> Does anybody else think that Narcissa was set up by
> Voldemort? Why would he tell oh-so-top-secret plans to
> Narcissa. She wasn't one of the people who NEEDED to know.
> Neither was Bellatrix, really.
>
> I think V told Narcissa the details of Draco's mission as a
> way of scaring her into running to Snape, and Bellatrix' job
> was to go along, pretendedly out of sisterly loyalty, but
> actually to observe Snape's reactions. If V suspected that
> Snape's Occlumency skills were a match for his Legilimency, he
> might choose to use Narcissa as a way making Snape let his
> guard down, and testing Snape's loyalty.

Voldemort is off-screen for most of book six, so we don't get much of a chance to observe him being sneaky. We pretty much have to infer it from what other characters do and say.

Troels explicated the triple-think involved:

> Snape himself summarises Bellatrix's views quite well:
>
> > **'You think he is mistaken? Or that I have
> > somehow hoodwinked him? Fooled the Dark Lord, the
> > greatest wizard, the most accomplished Legilimens
> > the world has ever seen?'**
>
> Apart from the whole question of the Vow, this chapter
> serves to show us how well Snape has managed to get back into
> the Death Eater organization. Voldemort trusts [Snape] (as far
> as Voldemort can trust anyone), which both Bellatrix and
> Narcissa acknowledges, and despite the ugly rumors among the
> Death Eaters, here represented by Bellatrix. But also
> Bellatrix is, in the course of this chapter, convinced that

> Snape is faithful to Voldemort, a turn-about that neither
> Dumbledore nor Snape ever managed to affect for Harry, but
> which Snape has managed to affect for Voldemort, despite
> Voldemort's certainty that Snape had turned against him (one
> might wonder how Snape managed to survive long enough to even
> speak to Voldemort).

POINTS TO PONDER: It appeared to me that Snape may have anticipated the possibility of swearing something to Narcissa and that he may have been prepared for it. Was that in a secret conversation with Dumbledore? In book six, we don't find out.

POINTS TO PONDER: Why exactly does Snape's hand twitch in the vow? is it at the thought of Draco failing, or at the thought of killing Dumbledore, or simply at the responsibility of the vow he is about to take?

This thought triggered a strong reaction from David Sueme that goes right to the core of the book.

> Well... I have a real problem with the "Snape is bad"
> storyline here. To me this is an incredible cheat. Remember,
> these are or were originally children's stories. To my mind,
> that makes certain premises inviolable - magic works, Muggles
> are stuffy and boring, you can eat as much as you like at the
> Feasts and never get sick, Harry is very special...

(David's wrong about this. Harry is repeatedly shown to be quite ordinary in the sense that he has a couple of strong talents – Quidditch, DADA—but is a regular kid in most respects. What makes him special are his choices.)

> Dumbledore is the smartest dude in the world and knows what
> he is doing.

(Is Dumbledore special because he's smart, or because he's good?)

> That has been a basic premise for five books/years and about
> 2000 pages. Now all of a sudden we kiddies are being asked to
> believe that the wise Dumbledore has been making a basic and
> crucial mistake in trusting Snape all along. I can't buy this.
> It isn't fair.
>
> I think Snape is being forced into taking this vow by his
> role as double agent. He is gambling his life, and DD's life,
> on a precise reading of the phrase "if it seems Draco will
> fail". As long as Draco continues to be the vacillating prat of
> the Hippogriff wound in HP3, it is arguably impossible to say
> definitively that "it seems Draco fill fail", or at least more
> definitively than at any point in the past. It's difficult to
> say what Draco may or may not accomplish, if anything.
>
> But all this comes to a crashing end for Snape when
> Dumbledore succeeds in talking Draco out of doing his job.

(In chapter 27, the Lightning-Struck Tower. Whoopsie, Albus!)

```
      Once Dumbledore plants the seeds of indecision in Draco's
vapid mind then Snape's gamble is a loser, his free will
effectively negated by the Vow, and he has no reasonable choice
but to execute Dumbledore, who has inadvertently maneuvered
himself into a position where his death is inevitable. One -
poison, Draco's hand or Snape's hand must kill Dumbledore as
Snape is not free to aid him.

      Snape's look of disgust as he kills Dumbledore is actually
meant for Draco. Dumbledore may have thought he found some
inner virtue in Draco; Snape knows Dumbledore found only
indecision and lack of determination. If Draco were at least a
determined villain then Snape would have been spared the
necessity of fulfilling the vow he took on a chance. But Draco
wasn't even that bad. His utter failure forced Snape into a
role he didn't want.
```

POINTS TO PONDER: Is it possible that Snape is frightened because he knows that Voldemort would not tolerate any additional oaths other than the ones that Snape has already sworn to the Dark Lord?

WHY I LOVE JKR: The way she totally knocks our socks off by shattering every preconception we may have had about what to expect in this book. The way that maternal love drives Narcissa to an extreme and quite possibly very evil course of action. The way Snape cold-bloodedly takes the vow …. And the way that we, the reader, are still kept guessing as to exactly the devil is in Snape's mind!

UNFORGETTABLE MOMENTS: Hands down: The Unbreakable Vow forming in the air between Snape and Narcissa.

Chapter 3 Will and Won't

SMART-ALEC SUMMARY: Dumbledore retrieves Harry from the Dursleys and gives them the ticking off of a lifetime.

POINTS TO PONDER: I wanted to learn more about Aunt Petunia, but we don't learn it here. JKR has told us she's not a Squib, and not a Muggle, so what is she? The only new information about Aunt P. in this book is the odd argument she has with Dumbledore about when Harry will reach his age of majority. Petunia coming from a wizarding family, surely knew at some point that in the wizarding world, Harry will have his majority when he's 17 ... so why try to make the argument for 18? Did she forget, or is she just being stubborn, or is there something more to it?

Troels Forchhammer guesses that the "more to her" is that

> [E]vidently her knowledge of the Magical world and in particular the fact that she hasn't forgotten it in all these years.

Louis Epstein thought:

> Perhaps wanting his freedom to do magic at their home to be postponed as late as possible?

That has a ring of truth to it ... perhaps there was some sibling rivalry and bad memories of Lily receiving more attention than Petunia because of her magic.

POINTS TO PONDER: Then at the end of the spat there's the moment where she looks "oddly flushed" -- is it because Dumbledore's criticism of their raising of Dudley stung home, or is there something else to it?

POINTS TO PONDER: Dumbledore asks that Harry be allowed to come back to Privet Drive one more time before he reaches his majority. At the end of the book, we learn that Harry does plan to do so, to honor Dumbledore's wishes. Will this trip to Privet Drive actually occur, and will it truly be important in book seven?

- Liz Reynolds commented:

> ... it may not be important anymore, the protection ends when he turns 17, which is only a few weeks away.

> I had taken Dumbledore's extracting that promise from the Dursleys as evidence that he expected to die within the year, but now I'm not so sure.

> It may be that they had to agree that Harry could come back next summer in order for the protection to be active in Harry's 6th year -- so he could still call their house 'home' during that period

POINTS TO PONDER: On reading about Kreacher's horrendous attitude, my first reaction was "Kreacher, what a frightful little thing!" When one imagines the havoc such a powerful, malicious magical "creature" ("Kreacher") could wreak ... one begins to understand why house elves are kept in such a state of wretched submission (sorry, Hermione).

Not everyone shared my anti-house-elf bias. As T. M. Sommers pointedly asked:

> As opposed to the havoc wreaked by powerful, malicious
> magical humans such as Tom Riddle?

A reader from Norway (the home of Ibsen's "Nora") commented:

> <style="sarcasm">
>
> Yeah! It's a preposterous idea -- like giving civil rights
> to women ... (no wait ... yes, that was it, civil rights to
> women, I mean, who'd be that dumb ...?)
>
> </style>

The discussion sparked some familiar arguments about whether "might makes right." Kish asked,

> Why keep house-elves in a state of wretched submission
> because of dangers such as Kreacher, and not keep human wizards
> in a state of wretched submission because of dangers such as
> Voldemort?"
>
> To which the obvious answer would be, "Because human witches
> and wizards, not house-elves, make the laws that govern the
> magical community." It's not right or fair, but it's the way
> it apparently is.

POINTS TO PONDER: Harry's instructions to Kreacher (go to Hogwarts and help in the kitchen) seemed a little slapdash. One would hope for a better thought out set of instructions ... but on the other hand, the more energy invested in thinking up stringent restrictions, the more vigorous and dangerous Kreacher's efforts to find a loophole to do harm. As it turns out, the presence of Dobby and the other elves at Kreacher's destination turns out to be an important mitigating factor on Kreacher's capacity to do damage. The built-in safeguard is that the house elves keep watch on each other!

POINTS TO PONDER: If we judge by the chapter title, the central development of this chapter is that Harry is recognized as Sirius's true heir, and inherits 12 Grimmauld Place. Although that's scarcely the most attractive place in the world to live, what with the nasty talking portraits, looking on the bright side, if Harry survives the series, at least he has a place to go. I was touched by Louis Epstein's comment on this point:

> I hope that the home of James Potter's parents is intact
> somewhere and waiting for Harry. It seems foolish to me for
> James and Lily to hide out where his family was known to live,

```
so I hope that the Godric's Hollow murder/destruction  scene
was NOT the home that Jams grew up in, and Sirius  spent his
pleasant moments of childhood in, rather than his  tormented
ones.
```

How else could Harry's status vis-à-vis Sirius be important? The mysterious "R.A.B." who signs the "missing Horcrux" letter at the end of chapter 28 comes to mind. If R.A.B. is indeed Regulus Black, then it might be important that Harry will have access to 12 Grimmauld Place.

POINTS TO PONDER: Dumbledore says to the Dursleys:

```
"I would assume you were going to offer me refreshment, but
the  evidence so far suggests that that would be optimistic to
the point of foolishness."
```

He is consciously addressing the precise issue that continues to torment Potter fans to this day: was Dumbledore foolishly optimistic in trusting Snape? Note that in this situation, Dumbledore is fully aware of the possibility that he is being foolishly optimistic, and takes practical action to meet his needs in any event. *Did he do the same with Snape?*

WHY I LOVE JKR: The great scene where Dumbledore ticks off the Dursleys for their treatment of Harry and Dudley, fulfilling every reader's dream of giving justice where justice is due. Troels Forchhammer justly calls Rowling "very brilliant to recognise that Dudley is actually the one who has the most to complain about ."

UNFORGETTABLE MOMENTS: Dursley: "I don't mean to be rude." Dumbledore: "... yet, sadly, accidental rudeness occurs alarmingly often" -- classic!

Chapter 4 Horace Slughorn

SMART-ALEC SUMMARY: Harry meets Horace Slughorn, the new teacher at Hogwarts.

POINTS TO PONDER: As Harry gets to experience Apparition for the first time, JKR takes the opportunity to give readers a quick primer on why wizards don't Apparate into each other's living rooms. It would be rude, and, anyway, many places have magical protection.

POINTS TO PONDER: We meet Horace Slughorn. We learn something about how high-class wizards can defend themselves as Horace creates an admirable illusion of a ransacked room with less than 2 minutes notice. The failing in the illusion? Horace didn't think of putting the Dark Mark in the air above it. This winds up being a fairly important check mark in Horace's favor, as later in the chapter and in the book we see him in a not very favorable light. Regardless of his failings, love for attention, etc., evil doesn't seem to come naturally to Horace.

POINTS TO PONDER: Steve Morrison contributed these nuggets:

> Dumbledore asks Slughorn what kind of blood he put on the walls, and the answer he gets is "dragon". So was that one of the twelve uses for dragon's blood which Dumbledore had famously discovered, or did Slughorn just find a thirteenth use?
>
> BTW -- Slughorn's name is apparently "an erroneous form of the Scotch word slughorne, or sloggorne, meaning slogan" according to http://dictionary.reference.com/search?q=Slughorn

POINTS TO PONDER: Harry's conversation with Horace is a nice piece of writing as Harry, quite guilelessly, says just the right things to make Horace see what he's missing in terms of "action" by staying in hiding.

POINTS TO PONDER: My "chapter title equals main plot development" theory works pretty well on this chapter because Horace Slughorn is not just the main new character introduced but (as we will find out later in the book) one of his key plot functions is to be the repository of a key piece of information that Harry needs.

POINTS TO PONDER: Dumbledore tells Harry to trust in his friends. Is this advice (which Dumbledore himself does not follow very well) part of Dumbledore's ~~death wish~~ master plan? In other words, even at this early stage in the book is Dumbledore prepping Harry for his own (Dumbledore's) inevitable death?

Troels Forchhammer offers a good common sense response:

> If you mean that it is part of his overall plan for Harry to teach Harry to strengthen his bonds of love (in all its

> manifestations, including friendship) and to teach him to
> include and rely on his friends, then you are, of course,
> right.
>
> If, on the other hand, you mean to imply that it is part of
> Dumbledore's plan in order to make sure that more people than
> himself and Harry knows about the prophecy, then I have to
> disagree very strongly -- if that was his purpose, he would,
> himself, have told some of the other members of the Order
> instead of (or in addition to) telling Harry to confide in a
> couple of other underage wizards.

I am compelled to agree!

POINTS TO PONDER: We learn that only two people, Dumbledore and Harry, know the full contents of the Prophesy. In other words, Dumbledore has kept the secret completely to himself until trusting Harry. Quite a compliment to our Harry!

POINTS TO PONDER: We learn that Voldemort has "finally" realized that Harry is a danger to him and has begun to shield his mind against Harry's observation. How does that work, exactly? Is it a one-way shield, or a two-way? Benjamin Esham offers a nice explanation.

> Think of someone looking outside through a window—if they
> pull the curtains shut, they can't be seen from the outside,
> but they can't see outside either.

POINTS TO PONDER: JKR observed in the Mugglenet interview that Dumbledore has no peers and is rather isolated. Is he capable of seeing that as a flaw in himself? I would say the evidence suggests "yes". Is he capable of addressing this shortcoming in a mature and effective way? Everything we know about Dumbledore the man— his humor, his insight, his charm, his woolen socks—suggests "yes"—but the record of his actions in book six is, sadly, inconclusive.

UNFORGETTABLE MOMENTS: "I do not think you need worry about being attacked tonight.' 'Why not, sir?' You are with me,' said Dumbledore simply.

Wo! Dumbledore is one cool dude.

Chapter 5 An Excess of Phlegm

SMART-ALEC SUMMARY: Harry visits the Burrow and gets caught up on the Phlegm situation.

WHY I LOVE JKR:

- "Phlegm."

- Troels Forchhammer liked it, too, but took it a step further:

POINTS TO PONDER: the Compact Oxford English Dictionary defines "phlegm" as follows:

```
/flem/

   + noun

   1 the thick viscous substance secreted by the mucous
     membranes of the respiratory passages.
   2 (in medieval science and medicine) one of the four
bodily
     humours, believed to be associated with a calm or
     apathetic temperament.
   3 calmness of temperament.


   —DERIVATIVES phlegmy adjective.
   —ORIGIN Greek phlegma 'inflammation', from phlegein 'to
burn'.
   <http://www.askoxford.com/concise_oed/phlegm?view=uk>
```

Troels commented:

```
     I think this nick-name is absolutely brilliant at several
levels.
     First of all Fleur's temperament is everything but
phlegmatic, but there's a beautiful alliteration in Fleur's
Phlegm ;-)
```

> Of course nobody manages to react to Fleur with phlegm,
> though phlegm would probably be the only sane way to react to
> an emotional tempest like Fleur.
>
> But this is also a question of French vs. English, and going
> by the usual stereotypes, it isn't the French that are known to
> be phlegmatic -- that fits much better with the stereotypical
> English stiff upper lip.

I thoroughly agree with Troels' assessment.

POINTS TO PONDER: The very female irritation with Fleur. Nice that there are no angels here! JKR does a nice job of describing realistic women who have petty and not so petty grievances with each other.

POINTS TO PONDER: I found it very scary to notice that Hermione only gets "exceeds expectations" in Defense Against the Dark Arts. Although JKR has established that Hermione is clearly a very talented witch, she has also given Hermione just the slightest subtle tinge of extra vulnerability. Will Hermione survive book seven? I hope so, but I have a feeling she is not going to make it. Ron seems sturdier somehow (perhaps because he's so %^*&^ dense!)

This idea prompted some spirited debate.

A.G. McDowell agreed with me:

> We have seen that Hermione sometimes gets flustered in a
> crisis (PS when Hermione identifies Devil's Snare but doesn't
> remember that she can produce fire any time she wants to. Also
> PoA, when Hermione gets fooled by the Boggart in her exam) -
> this is going to count against her in DADA - she probably
> revises so much because she knows she gets exam nerves, too.

Thomas Summers rebutted:

> That is unfair. She recognized the plant before the others
> did. She escaped its clutches before the others did. She
> recalled the plant's weakness before the others did. All she
> did was forget for a moment that she was a witch. If she was
> flustered, the others were totally flummoxed.
>
> … So you are saying that the only way to get an Outstanding
> is to perform flawlessly on every exam? I don't think Harry
> did that.

Her exam nerves are simply

> …because she is a very conscientious student.

McDowell pointed out that the fact Hermione is so bright means that she needs to have some counterbalancing flaws.

> Otherwise, frankly, the story would be "Hermione finally gets very annoyed with Voldemort. Hermione goes to the library. Hermione tracks down Voldemort, petrifies him, hands him over together with all his horcruxes to the division of magical law enforcement, and asks them not to bother her with the details as she has revision to do.".

POINTS TO PONDER: Harry's outstanding grades in DADA continue. Shirai noted:

> In OOTP, Harry is only TRULY comfortable with his DADA OWL, and gets a particular enjoyment out of performing well for Professor Tofty right in front of Umbridge, when she can't do a thing about it. Considering how totally useless Quirrell, Lockhart and Umbridge all were as teachers of DADA, and that by their fifth year, Harry's Hogwarts year had had only two years of really useful instruction from Lupin and from Moody/Barty Crouch, Snape is right to say it's amazing so many students in Harry's year managed to get an OWL in Defense against the Dark Arts. I wonder if any of the other students got an O in that besides Harry.

This is an important point.   Even though the DADA position is, apparently, jinxed (more on that later!), and Harry is by no means an official teacher at Hogwarts, he has managed to get "leave no child behind" results in teaching DADA!

POINTS TO PONDER: Fred and George Weasley make an entertaining appearance. They present themselves with an interesting new "accidental" identity as "defense industrialists" of a sort. Are they wearing white hats or black hats in this new role? Later events (Peruvian darkness powder) will make it a bit difficult to be sure. Richard Eney made a nice observation about their self-image:

> It's very telling that they got into Defense stuff "because it's such a money-spinner."
>
> Even leaving aside the fact that they didn't do it because people needed help, and didn't even think to claim that either:
>
> Consider other associations in the series with the word "spinner". =We have not seen anyone actually using a spindle or spinning wheel. We have seen lots of spiders, and the big magical ones are nasty.
>
> There's the mental image Harry has about Slughorn. [chapter 4] And there's Spinner's End.
>
> Fred and George are grey.

POINTS TO PONDER: Gabrielle Delacourt is "very eager" to see Harry. Could this cause (minor) problems for Harry and Ginny in book seven? Sharil pooh-poohed the concept:

> Hmmm, I think Gabrielle is several years younger--not old enough to offer real competition to Ginny. … Harry doesn't particularly like girls fawning on him--look at how he avoided

> Romilda Vane et al. ... He's also got more on his mind than love affairs.

Given this, I see Gabrielle as a source of minor comic distraction if anything.

POINTS TO PONDER: We learn that Arthur Weasley got a promotion to manage the Office for the Detection and Confiscation of Counterfeit Defensive Spells and Protective Objects. Is he being promoted over his head, or is Scrimgeour trying to influence Harry through Arthur. Efren Irizarry's bureaucratic analysis of the Ministry of Magic is a tour de force:

> [The creation of the office] suggests that Scrimgeour believed there was no existing office that could devote its attention to this specific area, even though several are related in some ways...
>
> The meat of the new office should come from Arthur's current department, the Dept. of Magical Law Enforcement. From the elevator [in OOTP], we know that its sub-departments include (but are possibly not limited to) the Wizengamot administration, the Aurors, and the Improper Use of Magic Office. I'm sure there are plenty of good leaders within the Auror group, but these guys seem occupied by rather more important work. The bulk of the Counterfeit Objects office deals with small stuff. (Molly did mention some cursed sneakoscopes from a Death Eater, but most of the job seems to be rather less nasty stuff ...plain old scams from run-of-the-mill crooks).
>
> So, that just leaves the Improper Use of Magic office to supply the bulk of the employees for the new office, and that is just one office of many, in one department of seven, within the Ministry. The Ministry is large, but it's not **that** large, so we're not talking about all that many employees. Arthur's old office is another source of employees for the new office. The Misuse of Muggle Artifacts office seems as related to the mandate of the new office as any.
>
> My point with all this is to show that it's a mistake to *assume* that Arthur is a dramatically inferior candidate to any other candidate--he may be among the best candidates. It's also possible that some or all of the better-qualified employees are already tied up in other, indispensable positions. Given the lack of data on Arthur's skill and the skill of others, neither of these lines of speculation are particularly implausible.

I know that I certainly have succumbed to the temptation to view Arthur as an amiable lightweight, but as Efren points out, this may be an illusion from Harry's point of view. Certainly Dumbledore and others at Hogwarts treat Arthur with respect, and Bill's competence and style must have come from *somewhere*.

UNFORGETTABLE MOMENTS:

- Mrs. Weasley seeing that *everyone* in her family is in mortal peril. This means both less and more than it seems. As JKR mentioned in an interview with cub reporters, almost *everyone* is in mortal peril.

    Trisha Mittal for the Hindustan Times India - My question is why is the Weasleys' clock set at Mortal Peril?

    JK Rowling: Mrs Weasley is right, if you don't know what I'm talking about, the Weasleys have a clock in which each of the 9 hands represents a member of the family and they point at things like at work, travelling and so on. Well at the beginning of this book all 9 hands are pointing at mortal peril. Mrs Weasley is right, she hopes that everyone is now in danger and she is correct. Well if the Death Eaters had clocks their hands wouldn't point at mortal peril. And the Weasley are what are called blood traitors; in other words they are pure blood but don't act that way. They consort and like Muggles. Therefore they are in the firing line, they would not be among Voldemort's favourite people.[5]

---

[5] http://www.quick-quote-quill.org/articles/2005/0705-edinburgh-ITVcubr...

- The very moving scene where Harry confides in his friends (while "talking to his fork"), and the effects on him:

    ```
    Harry did not really listen. A warmth was
    spreading through him that had nothing to do with
    the sunlight; a tight obstruction in his chest
    seemed to be dissolving.
    ```

- Very touching indeed.

Chapter 6 Draco's Detour

SMART-ALEC SUMMARY: Harry hangs around Diagon Alley and observes Draco Malfoy doing something sort of incriminating, but not exactly.

POINTS TO PONDER: The title, "Draco's Detour," is, of course, a reference to the means by which the team of Dark Mark "terrorists" gains access to Hogwarts at the end of the book.

POINTS TO PONDER: There don't seem to be many unexplained clues left over in this chapter. *Almost* everything in the chapter is explained later in the book. But there are a few niggling question marks. Liz Reynolds pointed out probably the most important one:

> It is never made certain whether or not Draco has the Dark Mark -Liz S. Reynolds

Maybe not significant in terms of the overall plot, but Draco's future may hang in the balance.

POINTS TO PONDER: How did Draco get away from his Mom? JKR doesn't show us, and it might give us some more insight into Draco's character.

POINTS TO PONDER: We learn in passing that Regulus Black "only lasted a few days" after deserting the Death Eaters. This doesn't seem to fit very well with the theory that Regulus is the "R. A. B. " who, we learn at the end of the book, has stolen a Horcrux from under Voldemort's nose. I don't remember it ever being set up that Regulus was Sirius's *super-brilliant, supremely- talented- wizard* brother, which is what he'd have to be to not only fake death at the hands of the D.E. but then at the end of the book put one over on Voldemort, big-time.

T. M. Summers argued the "talent" issue the other way:

> Harry is also not a super-brilliant supremely talented wizard. That a similar non-super-brilliant non-supremely talented wizard was able to get at a horcrux opens the possibility that Harry will also be able to get at them when the time comes. In other words, R. A. B. 's success makes Harry's future success more plausible.

Zgirnius pointed out how little we actually know about the events pertaining to the missing Horcrux in the cave:

> zgirnius: We know nothing about when the note was written, you could have the timeline quite wrong. If RAB is Regulus, it would have to have played out this way:

Regulus is a young DE who begins to realize this DE stuff is not all it is cracked up to be, and this Voldemort is just *not* a good guy. He decides he's had it with the DEs. But, he knows this decision may lead to his death, and he wants to do something to hurt Voldemort before he dies. He gets the real Horcrux and writes the note, leaving it in the Cave, where it is found some 16-17 years later by Harry and Dumbledore. Regulus leaves the Death Eaters shortly after this adventure, and is killed for his trouble a few days later.

With this in mind, maybe Regulus does not need to be a super-wizard. I think assuming he is a lightweight magically is unwise. Sirius is not a reliable person to believe about this, it's his little brother, and one he despised. But many relations of the Black family show evidence of considerable magical talent. (Sirius, Tonks, Bellatrix, Narcissa). Also, he could have had help. This is not my own theory, but people have proposed that Regulus could make Kreacher, the family elf, help him out. House Elves have some powerful magic of their own. Or, since Regulus was a Death Eater, he might have seen or heard something that gave him a clue how to proceed. Finally, he could have been helped by someone else who expected to live...and so preferred not to take any credit in the note!

Later, Zgirnius added:

He could have defeated the protections exactly like Dumbledore did. Maybe he drinks the potion, switches the lockets, stumbles out, and dies of the potion within hours or days, not having a Snape around to help him (and people suppose he was killed by a DE for leaving Voldemort). Perhaps the potion would be somewhat less physically debilitating to a young healthy man than to a very old and magically injured one.

If the locket "none of them could open" which the Weasleys and Trio find in 12 Grimmauld place in OotP is the real Horcrux, this would suggest Regulus died so soon after the trip to the Cave, or was so weakened by the potion, that he was not able to destroy the Horcrux as his written note suggests he intended.

Fair enough; Summers and Zgirnius could well be right.

POINTS TO PONDER: Where's Ollivander? I find it hard to believe he's gone over to Voldemort. He seems more like a determined neutralist. His role as an armsmaker makes it prudent for him to be absent until the war is won by one side or the other, lest they attempt to deny his services to the other side. (I love Neville's cherry and unicorn hair wand!)

POINTS TO PONDER: Narcissa to Harry: "Dumbledore won't always be there to protect you." How ominous is THAT?

Chapter 7 The Slug Club

SMART-ALEC SUMMARY: Harry gets caught spying on Draco and gets his ass kicked, big-time.

POINTS TO PONDER: The scene where Harry ponders Neville's life as the UnChosen One (like the UnCola?) is moving, even though it felt a bit like exposition for the reader.

Troels had a good observation about Harry's train of thought in this scene:

> One phrase that particular caught my attention was, 'The prophecy could have referred to either of them, yet, for his own inscrutable reasons, Voldemort had chosen to believe that Harry was the one meant.' There seems to be a recognition here that Voldemort's decision isn't entirely based on logic, and that it cannot be fully explained with reason -- the ways of the Dark Lord are past understanding.

Remember, though, that the comment about inscrutability is from *Harry's* point of view. Maybe in book seven we will find out that Voldemort's decision was more scrutable than it seemed.

POINTS TO PONDER: Great scene where Harry sticks up for Luna and Neville. For a moment I thought Luna was going to be Harry's girlfriend, but then her eyes were described as "protuberant" ... that seemed like a bit much, even for an author determined to defeat readers' expectations.

POINTS TO PONDER: Neville's cherry and unicorn hair wand is very touching ... speaks to his true innocence in the face of evil. Harry no longer has the same level of innocence (as is confirmed later in the book in a variety of ways). But Harry is more effective than Neville.

POINTS TO PONDER: Very cool that Ginny is invited into Slug's Club because her Bat-Bogey hex is so good. Just how good can Ginny be? Maybe we'll find out in book seven.

POINTS TO PONDER: It gave me the creeps when Zabini called Ginny a "blood traitor." Somehow the sting of that particular epithet is really awful.

POINTS TO PONDER: Why didn't Draco steal the invisibility cloak? Harry has amply demonstrated that it's a very useful magical artifact.

- Maybe Draco feels he doesn't need it--he was able to elude his mom at need, and he has his Slytherin cronies to help him get away with stuff.

- Perhaps he feels that Harry would go straight to Dumbledore, who would then take it away from Draco.

If appropriating the cloak was a bad option, then should Draco have used the cloak for an impromptu surprise attack on Dumbledore. We know that Dumbledore can defeat the cloak, but *Draco* doesn't know that, does he?

POINTS TO PONDER: A spirited debate arose over Harry's determination to spy on Draco. Some readers pointed to it as an example of Harry's superior perception and argued that it was helping set us up for the moment (later in this book) when Harry is more correct than Dumbledore in perceiving that Snape is a BAD HAT (as Ludwig Bemelmans' *Madeline* would say). Other readers argued quite the reverse. Igenlode Wordsmith wrote:

> One of Harry's increasingly annoying traits, throughout the series, seems to me to be his absolute certainty of things that turn out to be quite mistaken. The Potions book, for example. The visions of Sirius's torture (even I could work out long before the end of that book that listening to those dreams was a *really bad idea*, but did Harry listen to any of those who told him so? No, he did not!) Snape's guilt (/passim/). Karkaroff as criminal. Moody as ally.
>
> Harry is invariably convinced of his own correctness and then flabbergasted by a plot twist, and while an omniscient narrator who always knows best becomes annoying, so does one who repeatedly jumps to the wrong conclusion... it's getting to the stage where I'm starting to think 'Oh no, not *again*'. I'm sure there are lots of counter-examples, but the impression of Harry's recurrent bone-headedness is really beginning to irk me.

Troels then observed that the debate over "is Harry right to be so convinced of his own views" leads inexorably to a more fundamental issue:

> I do think that when we cut off all the excess baggage, we get down to a very basic question, 'Is this the kind of books in which killing "the wise old wizard with the beard" can be done as an act of loyalty towards him?

If Harry is an idiot (or, more charitably, simply an excitable young man who does not have information to which Dumbledore is privy), then Snape might be a good guy, and Harry's obsession with Draco is an example of Harry's compulsiveness accidentally working in Harry's favor.

If Harry is a shrewd judge of character, then Snape is a bad hat, and Harry's obsession with Draco is an example of his superior vision.

We'll find out which in book seven!

WHY I LOVE JKR: The way she destroys Harry's preconception, and ours, that the Invisibility Cloak makes him invulnerable.

UNFORGETTABLE MOMENTS: The scene where Draco spots, paralyzes, and brutalizes Harry, then leaves him paralyzed and invisible, was as chilling the nth time I read it as the first. It left me with two main thoughts:

- Harry is lucky to be alive.

- Ow!

Ann Williams pointed out:

> this is an interesting parallel to the scene near the end where Harry again is paralyzed and invisible by Dumbledore's command!

And quite few readers apparently shared the view that:

> Harry was an idiot.

Chapter 8 Snape Victorius

SMART-ALEC SUMMARY: Snape scores off Harry.

POINTS TO PONDER: The fundamental question of this chapter has become the fundamental question of the series: Is Harry more insightful about Snape than Dumbledore? A few stray thoughts:

Harry has the worm's-eye view, he sees Snape in daily life from the point of view of a student to a teacher, whereas Dumbledore only sees Snape when Snape is putting on S's best show for Dumbledore. (JKR has often shown the reader that it's in our candid attitudes towards others that we are truly revealed.)

Harry may understand evil better than Dumbledore because he has seen more of it first-hand as a child and suffered greatly because of it.

POINTS TO PONDER: The scene where Snape presents Harry at the Great Hall is odd. Snape says he thinks Harry wanted to make a huge entrance -- so instead he, Snape, arranges for Harry to make a very public and humiliating entrance, covered with blood.

What is Snape's motivation for this? simple cruelty? doesn't he run a risk of tipping Dumbledore off? Indeed, why doesn't Dumbledore question Snape's behavior when Harry arrives in this manner?

POINTS TO PONDER: When Harry learns that Snape will take the DADA position, he considers the idea that the DADA post is jinxed -- maybe tough luck for Snape! Question: if indeed Voldemort jinxed the post, should the jinx operate against Voldemort's allies?

POINTS TO PONDER: It is disappointing that none of Ron, Hermione, and Harry continue with Hagrid. It is also rings a bit false … when I was in school, I always stayed with the teachers I loved, regardless of their subjects. I think that's quite common. Surely one of the three would have stayed. I think the most interesting choice would have been Ron … now that would have given him an opportunity to grow in some interesting ways.

POINTS TO PONDER: One of the Aurors at Hogwarts is a Proudfoot–an *homage* to Tolkien?

POINTS TO PONDER: We see Tonks, looking quite the worse for wear, with a mysterious new Patronus. Has Snape guessed what it is? Troels comments:

```
'I think you were better off with the old one,'
said Snape, the malice in his voice unmistakable.
'The new one looks weak.'
```

```
I wonder if he has guessed the significance -- he obviously
enjoys deriding a junior member of the Order.
```

POINTS TO PONDER: Troels stretches a point to argue that Harry has more insight into Tonks than Hermione when Harry wonders whether the change in Tonks is strictly a result of the battle at the Ministry of Magic in Order of the Phoenix.

```
proving again to be her superior at reading other people (as
long as it doesn't involve his own romantic feelings, but
nearly all sixteen-year-old boys are idiots in that respect <g>
```

The "Harry-is-perceptive" crowd (which often includes me!) may have gone "a bridge too far" here, but it *is* a thought-provoking point.

Chapter 9 The Half-Blood Prince

SMART-ALEC SUMMARY: Harry gets a thrilling used textbook.

POINTS TO PONDER: The props given in this chapter to Neville made me wonder: what Neville be like as a grownup -- a highly proficient herbologist, also good at charms and DADA? Sounds like a crucial player in the environmental restoration in the post-Voldemort era. As far as we know, Voldemort hasn't been focused on environmental targets, but it's a near-certainty there's been a lot of collateral damage.

POINTS TO PONDER: We learn that Harry can after all take Potions (and pursue his dream of becoming an Auror) because Professor Slughorn is willing to accept "Exceeds Expectations" students.

Question: could Dumbledore have had this in mind? Is that why Snape was tagged for the DADA position? Is there a special reason why Harry needs to know about Potions? We are reminded on numerous occasions that Lily Potter was very good at Potions.

POINTS TO PONDER: The two old copies of the Potions textbook were left by Snape in the Potions cupboard. Is it possible that this was intentional? Did he do this knowing that two students, Potter and Weasley, would be added late to the class? It seems rather unlike Snape to leave his old textbook unattended.

POINTS TO PONDER: Crookshanks snarls at the Fanged Frisbee in the Gryffindor common room--is it important for any reason to remind us that he's a Kneazle? JKR has done this on several occasions, including a special call-out in a charity book, but owning a Kneazle has not really seemed to "pay off" for Hermione quite as much as owning a special magical creature usually does for the heroine of a children's adventure story (or, for that matter, an adult's adventure story). Book authors, as a group, seem to be highly pro-magical pet.

POINTS TO PONDER: As Snape takes up the position of DADA teacher, does he know or suspect that Voldemort jinxed the position? As an intelligent man who has been alive and conscious the last five and more years, he must assume that the position may be jinxed; what is his plan for dealing with the jinx? Or is he secretly assisting the jinx?

POINTS TO PONDER: Why hasn't Dumbledore removed the jinx? Is he capable of doing so? Has he chosen not to remove it because he feels in some way it ties Voldemort's hands, or weakens him by attaching him to something he cares about?

POINTS TO PONDER: Slughorn says that he took Felix Felicis at 24 and 57. Taking it at 24 presumably helped along his career as gilded connexion-monger.

What about the time he took it at 57? Why did he feel the need? Was that when Voldemort returned? Is it possible that the dose of FF at 57 somehow paved the way for his gift of FF to Harry several years later – and, in turn, paved the way for Slughorn's doing the right thing by providing Harry with the memory of the young Voldemort? Note that not only does Slughorn ultimately do the right thing, but he forgets it afterwards -- almost the best possible outcome for him! (If you haven't read Larry Brown's classic science fiction novel Ringworld, you must—and pay special attention to the character of Teela Brown!)

WHY I LOVE JKR: I love the Rumsfeldian moment where McGonagall compliments Neville, saying his grandmother should be proud of the grandson she's got, rather than the one she thinks she ought to have.

Is JKR unconsciously channeling Rumsfeld here?[6] It certainly seems that McGonagall and everyone's favorite Secretary of Defense are cut from the same flinty cloth (if cloth can be flinty, which it can't).

Troels Forchhammer commented:

> I was thoroughly charmed by McGonagall's warm kindness to Neville:
>
> > 'Take Charms,' said Professor McGonagall, 'and I shall drop Augusta a line reminding her that just because she failed her Charms O.W.L., the subject is not necessarily worthless.' Smiling slightly at the look of delighted incredulity on Neville's face, Professor McGonagall tapped a blank schedule with the tip of her wand and handed it, now carrying details of his new classes, to Neville.
>
> This, far more than any display of Animagic or any other kind of mere magic, is indeed brilliant ;-)

Well said.

---

[6] I realize that there is absolutely no chance that she is consciously setting him up as a target for admiration.

Chapter 10 The House of Gaunt

SMART-ALEC SUMMARY: How much fun is it to be a Gaunt? Not much.

POINTS TO PONDER: Trelawney "sees" Harry using a pack of tarot? cards -- "young man who dislikes the questioner" -- and dismisses it -- "well, *that* can't be right." Question: is this genuine divination? There are none of the hallmarks that accompanied her "true" prophesy.

POINTS TO PONDER: Marvolo called his daughter a Squib. Did he know he was wrong?

POINTS TO PONDER: Was any of Merope's magic involved in Tom Riddle's birth? "Give me a child who will make him love me..." Troels Forchhammer:

> It was certainly not used to keep the mother alive or to
> give the boy a happy life, was it :-/
>
> If anything, then Merope's powers may have been involved in
> shaping her son -- giving him the good looks of his father, but
> some of the madness of the her own father:
>
>> 'Now, as it happens, she did,' said Mrs.
>> Cole, who seemed to be rather enjoying herself
>> now, with the gin in her hand and an eager
>> audience for her story. 'I remember she said to
>> me, 'I hope he looks like his papa,' and I won't
>> lie, she was right to hope it, because she was no
>> beauty -- and then she told me he was to be named
>> Tom, for his father, and Marvolo, for her father
>> -- yes, I know, funny name, isn't it? We wondered
>> whether she came from a circus -- and she said
>> the boy's surname was to be Riddle. And she died
>> soon after that without another word.
>
> /If/ (and I certainly agree that it is unlikely in any
> event) any magic was involved in this birth, then I feel that
> it must be related to Merope's wishes: that Tom would have the
> looks of this father (name him Tom), the power of her father
> (name him Marvolo) and be a mystery (name him Riddle).

A brilliantly designed trifecta, worthy of JKR!

POINTS TO PONDER: What exactly is the mechanism for transmission of magical gifts? How is it that Merope, apparently an averagely talented witch, crossed with a Muggle, brought forth the supremely talented Voldemort? For the same matter, Hermione from two Muggles?

POINTS TO PONDER: Tom Riddle's Muggle love interest -- "Cecilia" -- have we seen her anywhere else?

POINTS TO PONDER: The black ring has the word "Peverell" associated with it. Who were the Peverells? What exactly is this ring? There was some interesting dialog on this score at the Sugar Quill. Nothing conclusive, but some tasty tidbits

> Perspehone_Kore wrote: Oh, and I was wondering about the Peverell crest myself. I don't think the name occurs elsewhere in the books. Given the way Marvolo presented the ring and the locket -- the Peverell arms as evidence of centuries of purebloodedness, then the locket to prove Slytherin -- I rather suspect the Peverells were a family that intermarried with Salazar's line, rather than all having been part of it, but I could be wrong; it could be a sequence straight back.
>
> I went looking to see if I could find any historical references to Peverell. So far I've found it as part of Plymouth in Devon, and as the surname of somebody William of Normandy gave a whole lot of land. The latter and his family may or may not have used a coat of arms which involved red and gold and a lion. I suspect this is completely irrelevant, but I was entertained.
>
> TDU wrote: Peverell was the illegitimate son of William the Conqueror (1066 and all that) - possibly his brother (William himself was illegitimate so this wasn't too big a deal). His family were given some sort of castle in Derbyshire (at Bakewell, I think but not too sure). There was a Peverell coat of arms (acknowledgement of nobility I think).7

POINTS TO PONDER: The story of the House of Gaunt brings to mind various scraps of memory about genetics and the danger of-breeding.

POINTS TO PONDER: Dictionary researcher Troels Forchhammer went to the Oxford English Dictionary and unearthed the following good info:

> gaunt + adjective 1 lean and haggard, especially through suffering, hunger, or age. 2 (of a place) grim or desolate in appearance.
>
> — DERIVATIVES gauntly adverb gauntness noun.
>
> — ORIGIN of unknown origin.
>
> I don't know what the Gaunts have suffered besides hunger and age (a house that had grown too old), but their house was certainly both grim and desolate in appearance.
>
> Even with Jo's uncanny knack with names it is rare to find one that is more fitting than this -- the house, in all its meanings, is definitely gaunt.

WHY I LOVE JKR: Merope's tragedy is genuinely heart-rending.

---

7 http://www.sugarquill.net/forum/lofiversion/index.php/t7131.html

Chapter 11 Hermione's Helping Hand

SMART-ALEC SUMMARY: Hormones and Quidditch.

POINTS TO PONDER: Hermione educates Harry on his new image.

> "Frankly, you've never been more fanciable … The whole Wizarding world has had to admit that you were right about Voldemort being back and that you really have fought him twice in the last two years and escaped both times."

"Fanciable?" Two thoughts:

- We *are* in England, not America.

- There's something of a disconnect between being "fanciable", as in "cute", and being right about a major world tragedy.

POINTS TO PONDER: Hermione is able to Confund Cormac McLaggen under the noses of a large crowd of watching witches and wizards without anyone (save Harry) noticing. A pretty nice piece of non-verbal spellcasting that serves to underline Hermione's skill.

Maestro Muten found this something of a stretch:

> I think JKR is making Hermione a bit too skilled for a 16/17. Or the others very very far behind the average. In the books you always see adults making any kind of magic, verbal or not, and even wandless stuff. And not just the most knowledgeable and ancient, even the youngest like Fred and George who can turn a knife in paper on the fly. You can expect a 4th-grade to Alohomora a door or Reparo a glass by just tapping or waving wand, and Harry is almost graduated and still can't cast wordlessly the spells in which he's very skilled. JKR, what did ya do?

I don't agree – I think JKR has her own reasons for making sure we realize that Hermione is skillful enough to pull her own weight in the Final Battle.

POINTS TO PONDER: It's emphasized that Harry and Ron are tall. I wonder if JKR's portrayal of them has been affected by the actors in the movies. Having the movies and the books written almost in parallel is quite handy as it mitigates many of the annoying problems that occur when actors don't look much like the beloved characters as whom they are cast.

Juvenal pointed out:

> Their maturity is more important here. The Trio [of Harry, Ron, and Hermione] are emerging (at different rates) as young

```
adults, and JKR emphasizes this in many ways:  for instance,
she usually refers to adult characters "striding", and she
applied this to the Trio too. There's also Scrimgeour's angry
reference to Harry as "Dumbledore's man."
```

POINTS TO PONDER: What is Ron really thinking and feeling? He gives a convincing impersonation of a not very bright, rather boorish teenager. But is there more going on underneath than meets the eye? This scene is a tipoff that maybe so:

```
"Anyone we know dead?" asked Ron in a determinedly casual
voice; he posed the same question every time Hermione opened
her paper.
```

Imagine for a moment what it's like to be a devoted member of a large and loving family, every member of whom is in "mortal peril." The Guardian had a nice para on this score:

```
     Some might feel a little like Ron Weasley when he sees
Hermione Granger reading the unreliable, indispensable wizard
tabloid, the Evening Prophet. "Anyone else we know  died?"
enquires Harry's bosom pal, with a "forced  toughness" in his
voice. Well might he ask, for the body  count has been
mounting. Just as Jane Austen's sixth novel, Persuasion, was
full of deaths, so is Rowling's.  It begins, in the non-magical
world of us Muggles, with  reports of murders and "dozens" of
fatalities from a  collapsing bridge (arranged somehow by the
wizard villain Voldemort). It ends with the notably unconsoling
funeral of one of her chief characters. In between there are
plenty more deaths put on by cunning and forc'd cause.⁸
```

POINTS TO PONDER: JKR forestalls many strands of fact-free plot speculation by having Hermione point out, in the visit to Hagrid's, that the entire Ministry stock of Time-Turners was smashed last summer.

POINTS TO PONDER: Very unpleasant how Slughorn snubs Ron when inviting Harry & Hermione to supper. "It was as though Ron was not present; Slughorn did not so much as look at him."

POINTS TO PONDER: It's established that Harry wasn't searched on arrival at Hogwarts, but everyone else was. But more importantly it's established that there's no way Malfoy could have brought a dangerous or Dark object into the school.

POINTS TO PONDER: On the "chapter title" theory, it would appear that the most important plot development in this chapter is that, by helping Ron win the job of Keeper, Hermione reveals something of her true feelings about Ron to Harry (and the reader).

---

⁸ http://books.guardian.co.uk/print/0,3858,5244854-108779,00.html

WHY I LOVE JKR: I found it particularly chilling to be reminded at the outset of the chapter that Harry still has the marks on the back of his hand where Umbridge made him write "I will not tell lies" in his own skin.

Chapter 12 Silver and Opals

SMART-ALEC SUMMARY: Harry catches Mundungus Fletcher stealing his silver, and an opal necklace nearly kills Chaser Katie Bell.

POINTS TO PONDER: Harry wonders "Where was Dumbledore, and what was he doing?" Although we find out many of the answers to this question later in the book, I don't think we find out *all* the answers until book seven.

POINTS TO PONDER: Harry explores the Prince's "self-invented spells." I don't think we've seen Harry invent any spells yet. Zgirnius points out that we may have seen Hermione invent one:

> Whatever curse/hex/jinx Hermione cast on the paper signed by all the DA members, that caused Marietta to break out...could that be a Hermione original? Whatever it was, unjinxing it was beyond Umbridge (though that might not be indicative). However, over the summer, wouldn't Marietta have sought out a Healer at St. Mungo's? Yet, she's still got the "Sneak" on her face... so that gives us a measuring stick for just how advanced a student the Prince was.

So perhaps Hermione and the Prince were at a different level than Harry. The Prince, with his plethora of self-invented spells, seems to have been more advanced than Hermione.

POINTS TO PONDER: The effects when Katie Bell is cursed are genuinely horrifying. Wizarding assassination is a frightful thing.

POINTS TO PONDER: Harry revisits the Malfoy facts with McGonagall. Hermione points out that what he actually said was, "How would I look carrying that down the street?" Note how Hermione is often used to get things straight for the characters. Not quite the equivalent of the sort of Bible where Jesus' words are in red, but Hermione's words have often deserved a little extra attention from the reader. Things are changing, though, as Troels pointed out:

> The changes to the group dynamics here are, IMO, very interesting. We're more or less used to treat Hermione's words in the first five books as very close to 'scripture' (only Dumbledore's words really deserve that status), and Ron's words as false (unless he was joking, in which case there might be a hidden clue in them), but now we see a much more complex picture. We know absolutely that Hermione was wrong with respect to Draco being a Death Eater, and we know that Harry was absolutely right...

Hermione's words are not Holy Writ. A. G. McDowell offers another angle:

> Another quibble - Ron - if not an authority on magic
> compared to Hermione - is - as the only one of the three
> brought up in the wizarding word - an authority on what the
> Wizarding community thinks about some issue. For instance, the
> treatment of house-elves, or the status of half-giants.

Discerning readers, pay attention not just to what is said, but to who says it.

POINTS TO PONDER: I found it both interesting and rather distressing that Mundungus Fletcher is able to roam about stealing things with such impunity -- he only fears Dumbledore. A wizard with ill intentions can do an awful lot of damage in this Wizarding world. Ard Rhi put this in a more realistic perspective for me:

> Mundungus seemed to fear Sirius, as well. Although Sirius
> nearly let him have the silver while alive, Mundungus stayed
> well clear of it. Not to mention Mundungus threw a neat little
> panic fit at the mere presence of Harry.

Very true!

POINTS TO PONDER: Mundungus's appearance in this chapter is the only bit of business that doesn't seem to have much to do with the Katie Bell/Draco Malfoy storyline. The details Mundungus's theft of something "silver" from 12 Grimmauld Place are not fully explicated later in the book. Could this be significant?

- Yes, especially if we believe that "R. A. B." is Regulus Black and that the Horcrux he stole is somewhere at 12 Grimmauld Place...

- Not necessarily. Ard Rhi pointed out:

  > Variation on a theme, more likely. Rowling
  > likes to remind us of what Harry has lost and
  > why he must continue. The theft of the silver by
  > Mundungus is just another reminder. His parents,
  > his godfather, his property, (later, his
  > mentor), and we still have book seven to go. I
  > got the feeling that scene was done more to show
  > Harry's depth than because of anything
  > significant.

Let's hope so. That sentence about Harry's losses was chilling.

Chapter 13 The Secret Riddle

SMART-ALEC SUMMARY: Peabody and Sherman take a trip in the way-back machine to visit Tom Riddle on his eleventh Birthday.

POINTS TO PONDER: Snape was asked to cure Katie Bell because "he knows much more about the Dark Arts" than Madam Pomfrey, per Dumbledore. I confess that I was a bit surprised by this. I thought Madam Pomfrey was a capable healer, and I didn't expect Snape to be good at healing. But, as we see later in the book, Snape is as competent at healing as he is at every other magical skill.

POINTS TO PONDER: Dumbledore tells Harry can "rest assured" that Mundungus Fletcher will not be making off with any more of Sirius's old possessions. But it also sounds as if Mundungus has successfully avoided direct contact with Dumbledore. So how did Dumbledore warn Mundungus off? Surely Dumbledore would have many mechanisms for getting that message to even a moderately talented wizard, but does it matter at all which mechanism?

POINTS TO PONDER: Caractarus Burke paid Merope 10 Galleons for Slytherin's locket. What a bargain! And what a cheapskate.

Gjw weighed in:

```
        Just a personal note: I've always found it reprehensible
when merchants take advantage of a person's desperation to
offer them a criminally low price for what they know is an
extremely valuable object. Some even brag about it. Capitalism
or not, IMO it's little more than theft.
```

POINTS TO PONDER: When Riddle says "Tell the truth!" to Dumbledore is it a spell?

POINTS TO PONDER: Merope's death is a riddle wrapped in an enigma – how can a magically talented person starve to death? Merope's skills, we are told, withered away with her broken heart. In other words, there is an intimate relationship between a person's capacity, and need, for love, and their magical talents. A proposition that Voldemort would surely deny, and Dumbledore affirm.

POINTS TO PONDER: Riddle's self-inventory of magical skills at 11:

- Telekinesis (I can make things move without touching them)

- Mastery of animals (I can tell animals what to do)

- Jinxing (I can make bad things happen to people who annoy me)

- Cursing (I can make them hurt if I want to)

We see *some* of these skills in full "flower" in Voldemort's mature life in form of the *jinxed* DADA position and the Death-Eaters' proficiency with the Unforgivable *curses.* We also see Voldemort exhibit impressive *mastery over animals* with his use of the snake Nagini.

I don't recall, though, seeing Voldemort demonstrate extremely powerful telekinesis spells—which is interesting, because telekinesis just happens to be one of Harry's best magical talents. Harry uses "Accio," a telekinesis spell, to great effect against Voldemort in both *Goblet of Fire* and *Half-Blood Prince.* In other words, one of Harry's magical strengths is the same as one of Voldemort's as a young man, which we have not yet seen Voldemort use as a mature adult. Coincidence? This, like Harry's skill at Parselmouth, seems to suggest that there's something to the idea when Voldemort's spell backfired, some part of Voldemort, or at least his skills and talents, split off into Harry.

POINTS TO PONDER: The Mad Scribbler asked a very sensible question:

> I was just thinking that there are
> two things that bother me about this chapter...
>
> 1. If [11-year-old Riddle] can do these things, even
> accidentally, why wasn't a Ministry owl sent to the orphanage
> warning about the use of underage magic, magic in front of
> muggles, etc?\`
>
> 2. If the Ministry doesn't punish underage magic before age
> 11, what kind of things did Harry manage to do that wasn't
> touched on in the books that would have driven Vernon and
> Petunia to drink?

Richard Eney explained away point #1:

> Underage magic before age 11 is considered accidental, and
> is commonly ignored by muggles, or explained away, as Harry's
> was: 'climbing on the school', probably 'spilling ink', 'the
> sweater shrank'. The MoM doesn't have to get involved.

POINTS TO PONDER: Again we see that Tom Riddle is very similar to Harry Potter: raised among uncaring Muggles, unaware of his own gifts until age eleven. Yet they are very different -- one a sociopath, one a caring individual.

POINTS TO PONDER: Dumbledore asks rhetorically: "Did I know that I had met most dangerous Dark Wizard of all time? No."

POINTS TO PONDER: Dumbledore makes sure Harry knows that Tom Riddle

- Wanted to be different, special, and notorious.

- Was self-sufficient, secretive, and friendless.

- Liked to collect trophies

Of these, the point about trophies seems least obvious from Voldemort's public persona, and is, of course, the most important for Harry to appreciate, since it illuminates the secret of the Horcruxes.

POINTS TO PONDER: At the end of the chapter, Harry notices that Marvolo Gaunt's ring is gone and guesses that it might be a mouth organ on a nearby table in Dumbledore's office. Dumbledore contradicts Harry's guess--"the mouth organ was only ever a mouth organ." Note, though, that Dumbledore doesn't rule out that the yo-yo and silver thimble also on the table might have been enchanted!

UNFORGETTABLE MOMENTS: When Riddle tells Dumbledore, "My mother couldn't have been magic, or she wouldn't have died." Moving because it shows that even the most dangerous Dark Wizard of all time was once a child with a child's way of thinking.

WHY I LOVE JKR:

- I love the way that Dumbledore & JKR demonstrate their understanding that sociopathy and domestic violence have their roots in power, domination, and cruelty. Dumbledore says Tom Riddle at 11 was "already using magic against other people to frighten, to punish, to control." Riddle's mastery of Parselmouth "did not make me nearly as uneasy as his obvious instinct for cruelty, secrecy, and domination."

- I love the scene where Dumbledore tells Harry not to judge Merope too harshly. "She was greatly weakened by long suffering and she never had your mother's courage." JKR & Dumbledore always offer such great and compassionate insight into human nature.

Chapter 14 Felix Felicis

SMART-ALEC SUMMARY: Ron gets lucky (or thinks he does).

POINTS TO PONDER: The fundamental mystery of this chapter: just how does Ron's mind work? Is he really an extremely capable Keeper beset by self-doubt, or an average Keeper who can temporarily psych himself into outstanding play? The same question expressed another way: is he going to pull his weight in The Final Battle?

POINTS TO PONDER: We see Ron scare the small girl who drops the bottle of toadspawn. Later, we discover that this was Crabbe or Goyle. Have we discovered *all* the occasions on which one of Malfoy's cohorts used Polyjuice Potion?

POINTS TO PONDER: I loved it when Ginny crashed into Zacharias Smith. We're seeing here that Ginny is very loyal!

POINTS TO PONDER: "Felix Felicis" was one of the chapter names leaked before publication and, like many others, I was fooled into thinking it might have had something to do with a cat …

POINTS TO PONDER: I'd like to better understand the nature of Hermione's spell with the yellow birds circling around her head. What type of birds can she summon? How big can she make them? What can she make them do? How far can she control them? As she develops her skill potentially quite a powerful spell! Imagine eagles flying around her head at a radius of a few hundred meters…

UNFORGETTABLE MOMENTS:

- Hermione saying: "if you'd rather I hooked up with McLaggen…" "No, I wouldn't," said Ron quietly.

- Harry's one-liner when he selected Katie Bell to replace Dean Thomas: "Harry had endured worse mutterings than this in his school career."

WHY I LOVE JKR: When Harry pretended to give Ron FF, it fooled me!

Chapter 15 The Unbreakable Vow

SMART-ALEC SUMMARY: Harry eavesdrops up a storm, but no one is impressed.

POINTS TO PONDER: Right at the first paragraph the mention of holly and its Christmas associations reminded me of Harry's wand, which is also made of holly ... the symbolism of rebirth, renewal, and sacrifice is so strong.

POINTS TO PONDER: It's always easy for authors to pander to the top-tier customers, the librarians who buy hundreds of books at a swoop. JKR may be pandering, just a bit, with the scene between the Trio and Madame Pinch.

> "What have you been doing to that book, you depraved boy!"
>
> "It's just a book that's been written on!"
>
> "Despoiled! Desecrated! Befouled!"

Yet note how there's always something passive-aggressive about the relationship between authors and librarians. Although librarians are usually portrayed with some affection, there's often this undertone of eccentricity, irrelevance, lack of perspective.

POINTS TO PONDER: Luna's description of Ron--"He says very funny things, sometimes, doesn't he? But he can be a bit unkind. I noticed that last year." I wonder if I'm the only one who's getting a bit tired of Ron by this point. Sometimes it seems as if Harry's closer to Ron's family than to Ron himself. I feel that Ron needs to step up and do something impressive in book seven.

POINTS TO PONDER: JKR's personal point of view on celebrity shines through most amusingly -- "if you were prepared to grant me a few interviews, say, in four or five hour sessions, why, we would have the book finished within months. And with very little effort on your part."

POINTS TO PONDER: Another reference to Trelawney and Firenze (or, as she prefers to call him, "Dobbin.") The references to Firenze in HBP have been just a little too pointed. I feel that JKR is poking me in the ribs and reminding me "don't forget about Firenze." I feel sure Trelawney & Firenze have an important bit of business to attend to in book seven.

POINTS TO PONDER: Another mention that Lily Potter is a great potioneer. "Instinctive -- like his mother!" says Slughorn. It seems that Lily's skill with Potions is important somehow, though it's difficult to figure out quite how. Could she have made a potion that will be important in book seven? Or does potioneering have something to do with the couple's presence in Godric's Hollow?

Gjw explained the "Lily is a potioneer" angle in terms of *Snape:*

> Given that Snape is 'the potions master', one would
> naturally think that Slughorn would mention Snape's talent at
> potions, but instead he continues to mention Lily instead. The
> importance of this, IMO, is that it provides a link between
> Snape and Lily, a common interest & talent that may have
> afforded them a reason to spend time together...

Zgirnius pushed the envelope on the Snape & Lily theory:

> Snape is to an extent responsible for Lily's death. He told
> Voldemort the prophecy. His later attempt to save James, Lily,
> and Harry failed because they chose Peter as their Secret
> Keeper. Presumably, he feels very guilty about this, and hates
> himself for having caused it. So, he looks for an external
> source of blame in order to allow himself to feel better. What
> better candidate than Harry? He looks just like the hated
> James. And also, there's this whole business about "Lily didn't
> have to die". It's all Harry's fault. Not because it is, but
> because Snape is not able to really face whose fault it
> *really* is.
>
> This would be similar to how Harry blames Snape for the
> death of Sirius at the end of OotP. If Harry had not been
> taken in by Voldemort and Kreacher, he would not have gone to
> the Ministry, and so Sirius would not have died in the way he
> did, coming to the rescue. So Harry convinces himself that
> Sirius came because of the cutting remarks about his lack of
> active involvement in Order matters which Snape made to Sirius
> weeks or months earlier.
>
> There could also be an element of jealousy. Harry looks a
> lot like James. So he's a constant reminder to Snape that Lily
> chose James, not him. A reminder of what he never had.

My thoughts? A stretch—but it *is* a logical possibility, given everything we know so
far. We'll find out whether there was any positive connection between Lily and
Snape in book seven.

POINTS TO PONDER: On the "Chapter title" theory, the most important plot
development in this chapter is that Harry learns that Snape has taken an Unbreakable
Vow.

WHY I LOVE JKR:

* I loved Ron's hilarious riff on "it's a free country ... I'm a free agent ... [Hermione] can't complain [after snogging Krum)

* I also loved it when Hermione said "I couldn't care less" whether Ron kisses Lavender. Hermione, always correct!

* There's a superb JKR one-liner when Hermione tells Harry about love potion plots: "It seemed extraordinary that Hermione's mania for upholding rules could have abandoned her at this juncture."

* "Ron's spectacular handlebar mustache" -- ha ha!

Chapter 16 A Very Frosty Xmas

SMART-ALEC SUMMARY: Holiday gloom at the Weasleys. No bowl games!

POINTS TO PONDER: The Trio goes through some more postgame analysis of the Snape/Malfoy confab. Harry: "No one's that good an actor, not even Snape."

It's interesting that the fate of the Wizarding world and Harry Potter is going to come down to J. K. Rowling's "theory of mind": is it possible that Snape could be so successfully deceptive, that he is a successful triple agent? Or is it a quadruple agent? I get to "quadruple agent" this way:

- Snape's original role as a "single agent" was Death Eater loyal to Voldemort.

- He became a "double agent" when he renounced his loyalty to Voldemort and told Dumbledore something so convincing that Dumbledore accepted Snape in his service.

- Snape now appears to be a triple agent, since, while pretending to work for Dumbledore, he is apparently working for Voldemort, consistent with his Unbreakable Vow.

- If Snape is a good guy after all, he is a quadruple agent, having renounced Voldemort, worked for Dumbledore, while pretending to work for Voldemort, but actually still working for Dumbledore all the time.

Party-pooper DarkD threw a bit of water on my colorful interpretation:

> It doesn't make him a triple agent or quadruple agent. He is at most a double agent. A 3rd party would be required if he were a triple agent. If he is on one side he is only tricking the other side.

Well, maybe, but I still like the sound of "quadruple agent."

POINTS TO PONDER: Isn't it a bit of a rip-off that in a book entitled "Harry Potter and the Half-Blood Prince" we never see anything from the point of view of the half-blood, Prince? (i.e. the 16-year-old Severus Snape).

POINTS TO PONDER: Lupin: Dumbledore trusts Severus and that ought to be good enough for all of us. Query: is blind faith a valid strategy for *anyone*? Especially when it is once removed.

POINTS TO PONDER: I liked Lupin's balanced assessment of Snape, remembering the positive that he made Lupin's Wolfsbane potion flawlessly every time.

POINTS TO PONDER: Another philosophical question: is Dumbledore's position vis-a-vis Scrimgeour really a reasonable one? Surely what matters now is mobilizing a grand alliance against the common enemy. Seems to me that Harry Potter and Dumbledore are fairly hard to please. They've finally got a go-get-em Minister of Magic in Scrimgeour, but they won't cooperate with *him, either,* just because he's going after some of the wrong guys (Stan Shunpike).

Would it really hurt that much for Harry to pop into the Ministry of Magic? Why not offer it in exchange for releasing Stan Shunpike and others from Azkaban? Harry is right to give Scrimgeour the stiff arm, since his leader Dumbledore is not available, but is Dumbledore really justified in refusing to cooperate with Scrimgeour? In another man, this might seem like grandstanding or empire-building.

Zgirnius did a nice job of stating the argument for Rowling's perspective:

> The disagreement with Scrimgeour seems to be that he is far more concerned about appearance than about results (or human rights). He wants to make his Ministry look good, wants to give the impression that they are making progress, whether they are or not. Harry, meanwhile, is just the opposite. He wants to get results and doesn't care much about how he looks as a result.

POINTS TO PONDER: Fenrir Greyback, there's a scary new character. He gets enough build-up that I think Harry will have to deal with him in book seven. Hey, maybe that's why it was important for Harry to get some beefed-up potioneering skills ... so he can make himself Wolfsbane potion!

Alex R. Mosteo chimed in:

> I bet on a Lupin/Fenrir battle. And of course Lupin will kick ass! But I agree that it's an interesting badass, even if appearing this late.

Zgirnius:

> Perhaps he should be stocking up on silver bullets... ;)

And an especially clever idea from Efren Irizarry:

> Oho. Let's remember that there's *another* person who could help take out Greyback, if it comes to that. Could this be Peter Pettigrew's chance to redeem himself a bit? God knows he could kill Greyback if he wanted to ...Pettigrew's silver hand would wipe the smile right off of werewolf Greyback's face.

POINTS TO PONDER: It's established that Harry's copy of the Potions book is almost 50 years old. Any particular significance to this date, I wonder? I doubt it -- the main point seems to be that of course Snape had to buy used.

Louis Epstein threw a splash of cold common sense on this line of speculation:

> Actually the critical thing about the age of the book is that it is A) after Voldemort left Hogwarts and B) before James and so forth got to Hogwarts.
>
> It thus dashes multiple suspicions of Harry's.

My suspicions are, I am afraid, groundless..

POINTS TO PONDER: "To Master, From Kreacher: maggots." Yuk. May I suggest to Kreacher, from Master, a special instruction: "you will always treat me with respect and kindness."

POINTS TO PONDER: Mrs. Weasley appears to understand the Tonks/Remus connection better than Remus himself, which is par for the course with the female contingent.

POINTS TO PONDER: Harry tells Remus that Tonks has changed her Patronus (or her Patronus has changed for her), but JKR keeps Harry and Remus's thoughts about the specific nature of the Patronus under the veil. I can't help but wonder whether Harry and Remus were thinking about the *same* large four-legged creature. If it was Hagrid, he would be assuming that Tonks' new Patronus was a hippogriff!

POINTS TO PONDER: "You're Dumbledore's man and through, aren't you." "Yeah," Harry answers. "Yeah" is such an American phrase it surprised me coming out of a British teenager's mouth. I realize British teenagers must say "Yeah" all the time, still, the "yeah" did a lot to establish Harry's evolving character.

Eric Bohlmann had a good point about intergenerational differences in language:

> Keep in mind that 42 years ago (33 years before HBP took place if you use the standard dating scheme), Paul McCartney's father was complaining that the Beatles should have sung "she loves you yes, yes, yes." He'd probably have fainted if informed that his son would eventually write "Sir" before his name.

And Blon Fel Fotch Passameer-Day Slitheen noted:

> The equivalent word "yea" is used almost 200 times by Shakespeare.

POINTS TO PONDER: JKR's position on the Ministry of Magic/Dumbledore debate seems to be that personal loyalty can and should trump "organizational commitment" (as one former supervisor of mine called it in a performance review carried out about a year before the organization showed its lack of commitment to *her*). This point of view is often found in fiction and makes for vivid conflict and attractively rebellious-but-loyal characters. Is it really the best message to be sending teenagers as they seek to make the transition *into* the world where a capacity for "organizational commitment" is an important part of maturity?

Of course, all fiction is subversive, as Alex Mosteo pointed out:

> I find specially entertaining (when looking for messages -- which I don't) the message sent by Fred and George: abandon your studies when you're near the end! Even if you are getting good grades! And they're two very likeable figures for kids. Go figure.

POINTS TO PONDER: On our "chapter title" theory, the most important plot development in this chapter is that it marks a low water mark in the happiness of Harry's "real" family, the Weasleys.

WHY I LOVE JKR: This feels like a very real Christmas holiday, like one I might have spent with my own family.

UNFORGETTABLE MOMENTS:

- Loved it when Fred turned Ron's thrown knife into a paper airplane.

- "We find we appreciate you more and more, Mum, now we're washing our own socks."—George--well said!

Chapter 17 A Sluggish Memory

SMART-ALEC SUMMARY: Harry bugs Slughorn to no avail.

POINTS TO PONDER: The "chapter title" theory works pretty well here, where it seems clear that "A Sluggish Memory" is indeed the crucial plot development. It's Sluggish both in the sense of being Slughorn-like and in the sense that Horace is slow to respond to the request for help..

POINTS TO PONDER: As Harry Floo powders to Hogwarts, he is spinning very fast and "catches glimpses of other Wizarding rooms"—if you slowed down the Floo spell, could you inspect Floo rooms like spinning a carousel?

Ken pointed out a fatal flaw in this theory:

```
No more romantic night by the fire.
```

I can't believe that J. K. Rowling would endorse a world without romantic nights by the fire…

POINTS TO PONDER: Hermione once again serves the vital plot function of correcting Harry's fuzzy memory: she reminds Harry that Malfoy threatened Borgin with a visit from Fenrir Greyback.

POINTS TO PONDER: When Harry tells Dumbledore that he told Scrimgeour that he *was* Dumbledore's man through and through, Fawkes lets out a low, soft, musical cry. The question I have is whether Fawkes responds to Dumbledore's feelings, or whether Fawkes responds to Harry's display of loyalty and courage? This may seem a fine distinction but I think it's important to understand Fawkes for reasons that will become evident at the end of this chapter and in the last chapter, "The White Tomb."

POINTS TO PONDER: Dumbledore offered the following after Harry's report on the Snape/Malfoy confab: **"I think you might even consider the possibility that I understand more than you did. … Let me reassure you that you have not told me anything that causes me disquiet."**

In other words, if we take Dumbledore at his word, Dumbledore is not caused any disquiet by the news that Snape has taken an Unbreakable Vow related to Malfoy's mysterious mission. How can this possibly be true unless Snape has provided Dumbledore with an explanation of the circumstances surrounding the U.V.?

Eggplant offered an important clarification to my question:

```
        No, that's not quite true. Dumbledore was not upset to learn
    Snape had told Malfoy that he had made an Unbreakable Vow, but
    I think he'd be amazed and appalled to know he really had done
```

```
it. Just before he was murdered Dumbledore told Malfoy, that's
what he would tell you, but we readers know he really did do
it.
```

POINTS TO PONDER: Phineas Nigellus endorses Dumbledore's view of Snape. Could Phineas do this if Snape posed a threat to Dumbledore? The painting people seem to be under some sort of constraint to act in Hogwarts best interest. Presumably Phineas has seen many interactions between Snape and Dd.

Gjw commented:

```
        The portraits are [not] omniscient.  They react the way they
    would if they were the actual people in the paintings.  The Fat
    Lady, for instance, is surprised and shocked to learn that
    Snape has killed Dumbledore. It's natural that a former
    Slytherin headmaster would defend the honor of Snape, as long
    as there was no clear evidence to the contrary.
```

POINTS TO PONDER: Dumbledore on Tom Riddle, superstudent: "Let us say that I did not take it for granted that [Tom Riddle] was trustworthy."

POINTS TO PONDER: Dumbledore tries to get Morfin released from Azkaban. Really, why bother?

POINTS TO PONDER: Phineas: I don't see why the boy should be able to get Slughorn's memory better than you, Dumbledore.

Dumbledore (paraphrased): I wouldn't expect you to, you grouchy old fart.

"And Fawkes gave another low, musical cry."

Dumbledore was not particularly happy at this moment, so Fawkes's cry cannot be related only to Dumbledore's mood. It seems that perhaps Fawkes's cry is triggered by the invocation of the power of loyalty and love.

UNFORGETTABLE MOMENTS: "We must try not to sink beneath our anguish, Harry, but battle on." Priceless.

Chapter 18 Birthday Surprises

SMART-ALEC SUMMARY: Ron gets poisoned twice in one birthday.

POINTS TO PONDER: The scene where Ron swallows the poisoned candies is nicely observed because of the very real mixture that Harry exhibits of sympathy and irritation with his friend. Throughout this book I liked the way that friendship is not romanticized … Harry feels irritated with his friends quite a lot!

POINTS TO PONDER: A bit surprised that the Anglicism "something that looked like cat sick" made it through the Americanese translator, but I suppose changing it to "cat barf" wouldn't have added much.

POINTS TO PONDER: When Ron winces at the sound of the name "Voldemort", Harry says impatiently to him, "Oh, will you get a grip!" I was surprised and disappointed that Ron couldn't say the name—underlines how much of a protected teenager he still is.

Blon Fel Fotch Passameer-Day Slitheen offered a great bit of perspective:

```
You don't have to be an advanced DADA practitioner to say
Voldemort's name. Here are the b1-6 scores for other people who
have said it...
```

Fudge, Ginny, Hagrid, Moody, Peter	1
Crouch, Quirrell	2
McGonagall	3
Remus, Riddle	11
Hermione	28
Sirius	36

I have a feeling Ginny will be saying the name a lot more in book seven.

POINTS TO PONDER: Awkward question, though: why don't Harry & Dumbledore call Voldemort "Riddle"? Isn't it giving lord Voldemort just the power he craves to even recognize this special and *completely made up* name that Tom Marvolo Riddle coined for himself?

POINTS TO PONDER: Harry points out that when he wants his friends to stand lookout, he tells them why. This respect for others is what differentiates him from Malfoy.

POINTS TO PONDER: Slughorn can be a good man when he is in a good mood—it is really quite Christian of him to invite Malfoy into the party.

POINTS TO PONDER: Again Harry is more perceptive than his elders when he realizes the vital split second before Slughorn that something is wrong with Ron on swallowing the mead. We see how Harry has been trained to hair-trigger perception and response.

POINTS TO PONDER: Slughorn to Harry on the bezoar: "You've got nerve, lad, ... **you're like your mother!**" Except from throwing herself to her death to save her infant son, which admittedly is a pretty big exception, what else have we seen Lily do that was nerveful?

Zgirnius pointed out:

> Perhaps another nervy action on her part was to involve herself in the Snape-baiting incident we saw in the Pensieve scene of OotP.

I guess marrying and reforming "bad boy" James could also fall under the heading of nerveful!

The bottom line is that even though we have finished book six, we still know very, very little about Lily Potter.

WHY I LOVE JKR: The suspense in this chapter was nearly unbearable as it looked for a moment as if JKR was finally going to fulfill our deepest fears and kill Harry's best friend.

UNFORGETTABLE MOMENTS: As the chapter ends we realize that the tragic death of Ron Weasley will be the centerpiece of book six ...

Chapter 19 Elf Tails

SMART-ALEC SUMMARY: Ron recovers. Harry has the house elves "tail" Malfoy.

POINTS TO PONDER: George observes that it was lucky Harry thought of the bezoar. But was it luck? If Snape deliberately left his Potions book in the cupboard for Harry to find, as we discussed at chapter 9 above, then it may not have not been just luck. Even if it was not planned, it may have been fated ... it's certainly ironic that the half-blood Prince's prized textbook should come around to help Harry in his time of need.

POINTS TO PONDER: Touching when Ron croaks "Er-my-nee" as his first words. Interesting (and a bit puzzling) that JKR doesn't give us a reaction shot of Hermione's face when she hears that. I wonder if the movie will. I hope so.

POINTS TO PONDER: "Half our family does seem to owe you their lives, now I stop to think about it," Mr. W said in a constricted voice. "All I can say it was a lucky day for the Weasleys when Ron decided to sit on your compartment on the Hogwarts Express, Harry."

Was it luck? Wouldn't the Weasleys perhaps have been a bit safer if Ron had never met Harry? Or would the clock's hands have turned to mortal peril even faster if Harry, alone and vulnerable at Hogwarts, had fallen prey to Voldemort/Quirrell? In any event, I question the idea that it was luck. It was a choice Ron made, one that was foreshadowed by his mother's nice treatment of Harry at the 9 3/4 stop.

Ard Rhi brought out that "choice" is a major theme of the whole series:

> As you put it, it was a choice. Molly chose to be helpful and nice to Harry. Ron chose to be friends with Harry. Their choices define who they have become and how they work together (or sometimes not in the case of Hermione and Ron arguing). While love and compassion has been a powerful theme throughout the series, another powerful theme is choice. Harry choosing not to be in Slytherin, the Weasleys' choice to be friendly to Ron, etc.

POINTS TO PONDER: In plot terms, the Dumbledore/Snape conversation that Hagrid overhead is obviously of huge importance. When Snape says "you take too much for granted," what exactly is he referring to? Snape's services as an agent against Voldemort—or Snape's commitment to fulfill his Unbreakable Vow to Narcissa, thus fulfilling Dumbledore's tricky master plan? Harry picks up on the fact that "despite all he had told Harry, in spite of his insistence that he trusted Snape completely, Dumbledore had lost his temper with him..." This does seem telling—Dumbledore not one to lose temper easily.

POINTS TO PONDER: Lavender treated as a figure of fun, even contemptuously, through most of the book, but is given one moment of insight in this chapter: "Friends, don't make me laugh! She didn't talk to him for weeks after he started going out with me!"

Ard Rhi commented:

> Her romance with Ron WAS a joke, so to speak. It was
> shallow, awkward, and lacking in any real communication. No
> surprise she was a topic of fun. But as Harry notices with
> women in this book, they can be VERY detailed, catty, and
> defensive. Hermione attacked Ron with birds and even used
> Cormac. Ron got some shots in too but if Cormac is any
> indication, Hermione was much more precise and vicious while
> Ron... just didn't get it.

POINTS TO PONDER: We know from JKR's Mugglenet interview that this was the last Quidditch match, which I find weirdly disappointing.

POINTS TO PONDER: Harry efficiently closes the Kreacher loophole—but lets it open at the end? "Just stick to Malfoy like a couple of wart plasters."

POINTS TO PONDER: This doesn't have anything to do with this particular chapter, but this is as good a place as any to wonder: the connotations of the name "Snape" are clear enough, but what about "Severus"? Did JKR choose this name to suggest a severe and serious personality, or to suggest someone who has "severed" his connections with his past?

This didn't sound right to Ard Rhi:

> It is possible, but it'd be very odd if she did. Rowling
> writes with "themes" in mind. Many of the female characters are
> derived from flowers, for example: Narcissa, Lily, Petunia,
> Lavender, Fleur, and probably one or two others. Along the same
> line, most of the male names tend to end in the suffix "-us"
> such as Remus, Sirius, Albus, Rubeus, Cornelius, and yes,
> Severus. To get two themes in a single name is possible, but a
> stretch.

Reader Phil offered some good historical info:

> I think it's down to the Roman Emperor Severus Septimus
> actually. Severus was actually used reasonably commonly 15th
> century Britain onward, right up to early 1900's when it fell
> out of use. As with quite a few of JK Rowling's names for
> characters.

I love people with historical perspective.

WHY I LOVE JKR: The very real feelings of grief and worry in Ron's hospital room.

UNFORGETTABLE MOMENTS: The classic opener: "So all in all, not one of Ron's better birthdays," said Fred. I'm beginning to agree with the poster who called Fred & George two of his favorite characters in all fiction. Can "Fred & George: The Apprentice" be far off?

Chapter 20 Lord Voldemort's Request

SMART-ALEC SUMMARY: Flashback to a meeting between Voldemort and Dumbledore.

POINTS TO PONDER: The low comedy with Professor Trelawney is very enjoyable and once again JKR makes sure that the reader remembers that she and Firenze are still at the school – a bit of business that could easily have been omitted except that it will be important in book seven! I thought it was funny when she tripped over her shawl.

POINTS TO PONDER: Dumbledore's attitude towards Divination interests me: causes "much more trouble than I could have foreseen," "never having studied it myself." A bit surprising that Dumbledore, who is such a polymath, never studied the subject at all. His basic attitude seems to be that it's all hokum, except when it isn't.

POINTS TO PONDER: As I reread the passage with Dumbledore reprimanding Harry for his lame efforts to get the memory from Slughorn, I felt myself feeling a bit sorry for Harry. After all, Dumbledore is the adult, and Slughorn is his peer (and employee). Shouldn't it really be Dumbledore's responsibility? Especially since it turns out later in the book that underneath it all Dumbledore's real motivation is that he thinks Harry is the person best situated to emotionally manipulate Slughorn into revealing the memory. Seeing an adult pressure a minor into manipulating another adult is not especially edifying … it underlines the depth of Dumbledore's desperation. Not something he would do unless the need was so great.

Igenlode asks a very good question which underlines that we don't really understand what Dumbledore was actually doing in book six.

> But why *is* the need so great? Dumbledore has already located and destroyed one of the Horcruxes, so he must surely know already what Voldemort did to obtain immortality. All the memory seems to give is an guess at how many Horcruxes he still has to seek out... but this is vital information, I suppose (it would be very embarrassing to have Voldemort cornered and vulnerable only to discover that, instead of being defeated, he disappears into a puff of smoke and goes back to being a bodiless menace!)

Some thought I was overreaching with this line of argument, and I don't disagree. I'm not saying that Dumbledore is a manipulative scuzball. I'm just pointing out that sometimes, if you look closely at what the characters are doing, it's subject to a more skeptical interpretation than is offered by either the viewpoint character (Harry) *or* J. K. Rowling.

POINTS TO PONDER: Tom Riddle's visit to Dumbledore's office is a great scene and very thought provoking. I was struck by the similarity between Harry and Riddle, both more attached to Hogwarts than any other place, their home, where they've both been happiest. I have a feeling that The Final Confrontation will take place on the grounds of Hogwarts.

POINTS TO PONDER: I wonder what special powers Helga Hufflepuff's mug has. Presumably have something to do with the Hufflepuffian qualities of friendship, hard work, and so on.

Richard Eney suggested:

> Nurturing, maybe. The series is full of grail images.

POINTS TO PONDER: We know a bit more about the powers of Slytherin's locket – whatever they are, they don't include anything to do with giving the wearer health or financial well-being, since its last owners, the Gaunts, were notably unhealthy and poor. Perhaps it enhanced Merope's powers of persuasion and enchantment…

POINTS TO PONDER: Dumbledore seems to have done an awful lot of tracking down witnesses and extracting memories. That seems to be par for the course for a high-class wizard – similarly, Voldemort spends much of his time running around creating false memories. This "memory modification" mode of high wizardry does leave some room for "R. A. B." at the end of the book to be someone who has been present all along, but skillfully hiding his presence. Unfortunately, Harry doesn't seem to be especially good at mind-oriented magics … he will have to rely on other techniques to get the crucial 411 about the Horcruxes in book seven.

POINTS TO PONDER: The convo between Riddle and Dumbledore is classic. Dumbledore is great at telling people off in a calm cool and collected manner. I wish I could have that presence of mind when I am in such situations!

POINTS TO PONDER: At the end where Dumbledore asks Voldemort's purpose, we never get a straight answer. So what exactly was Voldemort's purpose? Why did he want the job at Hogwarts?

POINTS TO PONDER: The existence of a jinx against the DADA position is, in my mind, firmly established by Dumbledore comment at the end of the chapter that the subsequent history of the DADA post "proves" that Riddle was after the DADA job.

So, yes, Voldemort wanted the DADA post … but why, exactly? His followers today seem to regard the discipline as a joke. Yes, it's a good recruiting post, but is there anything more to it? Is it possible that the person who is teaching DADA at Hogwarts has any special magical privileges while within the bounds of Hogwarts?

WHY I LOVE JKR: The contrast between the cool, collected, open Dumbledore and the cool, closed, menacing Riddle is fascinating.

UNFORGETTABLE MOMENTS: Riddle's "smeared" appearance is chilling.

Chapter 21 The Unknowable Room

SMART-ALEC SUMMARY: The Unknowable Room isn't kidding around, it's *really* unknowable.

POINTS TO PONDER: I found it interesting that Harry disagreed in his essay with Snape on the best way to tackle dementors.

Igenlonde made some interesting observations on this score:

```
     If there's one thing Harry is probably the most expert on of
anyone at  Hogwarts, it's dealing with Dementors :-)  And Snape
himself most certainly has a history of disagreeing with Harry
and friends in lessons 'purely for spite'!

     But what I (and others) really want to know, is just what
*does* Snape  teach as the best way to tackle Dementors? And
why, given the massive  build-up for 'Snape must never be
allowed the DADA job' and the  emphasis on this subject in
every other book to date, do we hear next  to nothing about
Snape's lessons now that he finally does have the post?

     (Well, I can guess the answer to that one—not enough space,
too many  other (snogging-related ;-p) plot threads—but I still
found it  disconcerting.)
```

The point about the excess of snogging-related plot threads is well taken...

POINTS TO PONDER: Am I the only one who thinks it's a bit of overkill to send Mundungus (or *anyone*) to Azkaban? Even with the dementors gone. Kish pointed out:

```
     The dementors are gone from Azkaban, remember?  Although I'd
certainly agree (if you would say this—if not, I'll have to
settle for agreeing with myself :-p) that when they were there,
sending /any/ prisoners to Azkaban constituted a massive human
rights violation and showed how far behind the Muggle world the
wizard world is in some moral ways.
```

I'd like to see the Hague take on Voldemort.

POINTS TO PONDER: When the trio is reading the newspaper it mentions that Octavius Pepper has vanished. He doesn't seem to have been mentioned elsewhere in the series. Throw-away character, or coming back?

POINTS TO PONDER: I would like to have seen Neville's reaction to the nine-year-old boy who was Imperius Cursed into trying to kill his grandparents. (And, by the way, why exactly is a 9yo who was Imperiused under arrest at all?)

POINTS TO PONDER: Snape provides another refresher on Inferi, setting us up for their key role in chapter 26.

POINTS TO PONDER: I like that Myrtle sees (Draco) as human, sensitive, bullied. Draco is such a figure of evil in the books (as differentiated from the movies or in fanfic) that it's good to remember he's still a youth.

POINTS TO PONDER: Harry scaring Goyle is hilarious. I hope the movie shows Goyle turn back into himself, the joke is even funnier with the visual of the fairly humungous and talented actor Joshua Hardman.

POINTS TO PONDER: Tonks' appearance here feels awfully random. It's as if she wandered in from the green room and forgot she was on stage.

POINTS TO PONDER: "Goading Myrtle seemed to have put fresh heart into Ron." Tonks is "cracking up." Again with the sarcasm, Ron. I'm getting tired of it. Apparently so was JKR as she gives Hermione a priceless score at the end of the chapter, tweaking Ron about his joke falling flat in front of Madam Rosmerta.

Ard Rhi had a more forgiving, and insightful, view of Ron:

> Ron also has unusual perceptions. Unlike Myrtle, it is less because he doesn't want to and more because he just doesn't have the depth of understanding. For all Ron's supposed flaws as he sees them, he is much more sheltered than Hermione or Harry or other characters. His innocence is both his best characteristic and his worst. Ron has his family, unlike Harry. He isn't a walking target for his blood like Hermione. He's not old enough or concerned enough to appreciate relationship issues like Cho or Tonks. That last one comes back to bite him in the ass when he has to deal with Lavender.
>
> The flip side of it is it makes him so much more sympathetic to people who do have those issues. Rowling even comments on the remarkable strength of their friendship in that Harry can tell Ron virtually anything and Ron will be right by his side, regardless.
>
> I don't think Rowling gave Ron the tweaking for his sarcasm... it's her character after all. She gave it to underscore the friction specifically between Hermione and Ron.

Blon Fel Fotch Passameer-Day Slitheen had a far less forgiving, and indeed, sinister perspective.

> Well, I have my suspicions about the Weasleys - for all that they appear to be blood traitors, their family is quite intact; while the McKinnons, the Prewetts, the Potters, and the Boneses have almost been wiped out.

Chapter 22 After the Burial

Smart-Alec summary: Ron comes up with the idea for Harry to "get lucky!" Ron pulls his weight for once!

Points to Ponder: Interesting that Harry was saving his Felix Felicis for Ginny ...

Points to Ponder: Hermione has a moment of real moral authority when she says "It's all about stopping Voldemort isn't it? These dreadful things that are happening are all down to him."

Points to Ponder: When Harry takes the Felix Felicis, interesting to see that he has at least 2/3 of it left. That's two giant plot holes that JKR can write herself out of in book seven! Again I'm wondering if it was really plausible for Slughorn to give this stuff away as part of a class, if there was not perhaps some unseen force acting on him ... perhaps Felix Felicis itself? Interesting that "Felix" is personified.

Points to Ponder: Interesting that the first thing that happens after Harry takes Felix is that his exit under the invisibility cloak leaving Ron & Hermione apparently alone together starts a fight between Lavender and Ron. Apparently Felix construes Harry's "luck" rather broadly to include the welfare and amity of his two best friends!

Points to Ponder: "Filch had forgotten to lock the front door..." —did he forget *before* or *after* Harry took Felix?

Points to Ponder: Slughorn's good character comes through in several ways in this chapter. I liked it when he said "I know Dumbledore trusts Hagrid to the hilt, so he can't be up to anything very dreadful." So many others have failed to trust Hagrid!

Down at Hagrid's Slughorn gives Aragog a great send-off. "Farewell, Aragorn, King of Middle-Earth ..." er, I mean, "Farewell, Aragog, king of arachnids." Slughorn really does the occasion justice! That's one good thing about status-focused people like Slughorn, they do have a sense of the positive value of ceremony.

Ard Rhi agreed:

```
        Slughorn really does represent the best in Slytherin. He is
    greedy, fussy, and soft... but not malicious or insecure like
    others.
```

Slytherin really does tend to get the short end of the stick.

POINTS TO PONDER: Felix tells Harry to stay sober and get Slughorn drunk. Then Felix tells Harry to say he "forgot" that Slughorn liked Lily. Felix tells Harry Slughorn will remember none of this in the morning. Felix gives very specific advice!

```
     I think Rowling lets Harry personify Felix a bit much. But
that's part of  the fun of the chapter. In this case, Felix is
specific but that's not  exactly new. Oft times people think to
themselves as if they were separate  people and we give
ourselves specific advice. We ask ourselves if we made a
proper choice and we'll tell ourselves yes and why. Felix did
similar.
```

POINTS TO PONDER: Who the devil invented this incredibly powerful potion?

Blon Fel Fotch Passameer-Day Slitheen had yet another enigmatic, unprovable, and thought-provoking observation:

```
     I'm quite sure that Felix telling Harry what to do is a much
closer approximation to what is really going on in this book,
than it being the Luck Potion which so many readers have
gullibly accepted.
```

POINTS TO PONDER: There seems to be a bit of a generation gap with regard to the name Felix, with some people below a certain age finding it hard to believe "Felix" is an actual name. The collective consciousness set this misunderstanding to rest:

- Felix Mendelssohn, famous composer.

- Felix Klein, inventor of the eponymous bottle (make a moebius strip, then join the edges. Presto! You have a "Klein Bottle")

- Felix Bloch, co-winner of the Nobel Prize in Physics 1952. Felix Frankfurter, Supreme Court Justice Felix Brannagan, Medal of Honor recipient

- 2nd Lt. Ferdinand Maurice Felix West and Captain Edward Felix West, Victoria Cross recipients.

- Felix Leiter, James Bond's CIA contact.

- Felix Unger, the value-added (fussy) half of "The Odd Couple"!

POINTS TO PONDER: Slughorn says Lily was "Very brave ... very funny..." I sure hope we get to meet Lily in some real detail in book seven!

Harry asks "are you scared Voldemort will find out you helped me?"

I think it's to Slughorn's credit that it seems the real reason for his reluctance is not fear but shame. "I think I may have done great damage that day ... Just don't think too badly of me once you've seen it!"

WHY I LOVE JKR: A great and pivotal chapter.

UNFORGETTABLE MOMENTS: I loved the image of Aragog lying on its back, "its legs curled and tangled …", and then when Hagrid threw him into the grave and he "hit bottom with a horrible, rather crunchy thud!"

Chapter 23 Horcruxes

SMART-ALEC SUMMARY: Harry and Dumbledore watch an episode of "Tom Riddle, Master Brown-noser."

POINTS TO PONDER: When Harry returns to Hogwarts, the Felix Felicis is wearing off … so does he immediately revert to his normal "luck quotient"? Harry seems to be something of a special case with several "standard deviations" away from normal luck – for good and bad (having his mom save his life from deadliest Dark Wizard in all history; having his mom die while doing so; being "chosen" by Voldemort, yet surviving multiple encounters with Voldemort; drawing the Dursleys as a host family, yet being protected by their magic throughout his youth). Indeed in Harry's case one might almost wonder if Felix actually tends to *"smooth out"* Harry's normally wild luck swings.

POINTS TO PONDER: Dumbledore looks "stunned" when Harry reports success on the Slughorn front. Then says "I knew you could do it." Ok, did you know Harry could do it, or not? What was your "plan B" if Slughorn wouldn't dish to Harry?

POINTS TO PONDER: Riddle tells Slughorn he didn't think politics would "suit him". Here's a first, a megalomaniac who doesn't want to be a politician. Go figure.

POINTS TO PONDER: One wonders if Riddle came across the term "Horcrux" in the same book that Hermione did, or whether he had already discovered non-Hogwarts sources of Dark Magic lore by that time? Where would a Hogwarts student go to find Dark lore? Off-campus during break, one supposes.

POINTS TO PONDER: Loved it when Harry recognized another master wheedler at work, watching Riddle wheedle info out of Slughorn.

POINTS TO PONDER: I liked it when Slughorn looked at Riddle "as though he had never seen him plainly before." Nice that Slughorn has the insight to realize that Riddle is deeply disturbed and deeply dangerous. Perhaps it's his failure to act on this insight – which as far as he knew, he alone had experienced – that causes him the greatest shame in later years. From this moment of recognition on, all the subsequent deaths at Voldemort's hands can be laid at Slughorn's doorstep.

POINTS TO PONDER: Ok, the diary was a Horcrux, but what was scariest was that it was a *spare* Horcrux intended for use as a weapon.

Alex Mosteo found this:

> A fishy point in the plot, IMHO. What's the point in making the most magical number of parts with your soul if one of these

is going to be lost? Though excusable if we can believe that nobody would suspect the diary involvement.

POINTS TO PONDER: He made seven Horcruxes? Not seven, six, because Riddle still has a fragment of soul.

POINTS TO PONDER: Just for the record: JKR is encouraging Harry, Dumbledore, and everyone else make a big-ass ol' *assumption* here that there are seven Horcruxes. We don't have any actual proof that it's seven. Riddle might have wanted to be the only wizard ever with eight Horcruxes. That would certainly throw a spanner in Harry's plans for book seven!

POINTS TO PONDER: Dumbledore destroyed Marvolo's ring … "and a terrible curse there was on it too…" Dumbledore only saved by Snape's timely action when he returned to Hogwarts. Here's yet another action very tough to explain in terms of Snape as 100% bad guy… if you're a secret Death Eater, why not let Dumbledore die?

Gjw explained it this way:

> Because not treating him would have alerted Dumbledore to the fact that Snape wasn't loyal. Then Snape would have had to try to kill him, something he apparently didn't intend to do until Voldemort told him to... After all, he's had a decade during which he could have killed Dumbledore when his back was turned... He was a "sleeper agent" who hadn't yet been "awakened"...

A sleeper agent who *was very deeply* asleep…

POINTS TO PONDER: Great and very helpful scene where Dumbledore confirms that Horcrux 3 is Slytherin's locket, Horcrux 4 is Hufflepuff's cup, Horcrux 5 is Nagini, and Horcrux 6 is either something from Ravenclaw or a Gryffindor object *not* the sword. That Horcrux 6 is not Gryffindor's sword seems confirmed by its role in *Chamber of Secrets.* If Gryffindor's sword were a Horcrux—which seems absurd on the face of it—surely it would have helped out its fellow Horcrux somehow, and it didn't.

POINTS TO PONDER: Am I the only one who has trouble accepting that Nagini is a Horcrux? Something about that just seems wrong to me. I can't fathom why Riddle would put a part of his soul in something mortal. Also, the other objects are immortal treasures, a snake, however cool for a Parseltongue speaker, just isn't up to the same standard.

POINTS TO PONDER: We haven't really seen the inner workings of either Ravenclaw or Hufflepuff in the first six books … we've only seen a few stock characters – I hope JKR goes into the inner workings of both houses at some length in book seven.

POINTS TO PONDER: Dumbledore observes "I am sure Voldemort was intending to make his final Horcrux with your death, Harry." But we know that Voldemort was pretty much out of action from then until *Philospher's Stone*. So it sure would seem that Horcrux 7 *was* made in the attack on Harry ... so how could it be anything other than Harry or his scar?

POINTS TO PONDER: We don't know exactly how the Horcrux creation spell works, but it seems likely it's carried out simultaneous with and contingent on the completion of the Avada Kevadra spell... so when Lily's motherly love spell blocked the AK, where did the Horcrux creation spell go? Can we say "Harry the Horcrux"?

Ard Rhi told me firmly:

> No, we can't. THAT is a big assumption. Slughorn clearly
> says that the act of murder is what rips the soul. THEN the
> dark wizard uses magic to take advantage of the tear. That
> implies a second spell or ritual. You're presuming that horcrux
> creation is simple, quick, and carried with a death
> spell when none of that is demonstrated.
>
> Further, Voldemort has tried possessing Harry and found it
> painful. For a piece of Voldemort's soul to reside within Harry
> would contradict why love protects Harry to begin with. It's
> not impossible for the "Harry Horcrux" theory to be true, but
> it needs to be a bit better supported than that.

Sound points.

POINTS TO PONDER: Lucius Malfoy secretly glad to be in Azkaban: indeed! I almost want to join him there, I'm so scared of book seven.

POINTS TO PONDER: Great point about what Harry saw in the Mirror of Erised and how few wizards could have seen the same thing.

POINTS TO PONDER: The point about being dragged into the arena versus walking in with your head held high fell a bit flat for me, as the first thing that comes to my mind is the Roman Coliseum, and there I'm really not quite sure it does make much difference whether you walked in head high. Hope Harry's not heading for one of those Lions 1, Christians 0 moments.

WHY I LOVE JKR: The unfolding of a profound and ominous mystery made this a profoundly satisfying chapter.

UNFORGETTABLE MOMENTS:

- Loved it when Harry could scarcely restrain himself from saying "Big deal" about his power to love.

- Great moment when *all* the old headmasters are awake and listening on Harry's conversation with Dumbledore.

Chapter 24 Sectumsempra

SMART-ALEC SUMMARY: Harry does a major oopsie.

POINTS TO PONDER: Lavender glares at Hermione ... Ron looks "immensely guilty" ... this is about as good as it gets for Lavender from here on out.

POINTS TO PONDER: JKR does some back-pedaling to dial back the usefulness of Felix Felicis by having Harry realize that the stuff is fiendishly complex and takes six months to brew. Hermione also points out that you can't rely on luck to defeat an experienced wizard.

POINTS TO PONDER: Harry is *still* tempted to take a slug of Felix to "tweak the circumstances" re Ginny.

POINTS TO PONDER: JKR sounds pretty bored with Quidditch: "The run-up to this crucial match had all the usual features ..." one can almost finish the sentence "blah, blah, blah."

POINTS TO PONDER: Tremendous scene with Malfoy in the bathroom. I was horrified and shamed at the effect of Harry's Sectumsempra spell on Malfoy. Considering this it is rather amazing that Harry still has the nerve? moxie? presence of mind? to hide his copy of his potions book from Snape.

I liked the moment when Harry thinks about the book "as though a beloved pet had turned suddenly savage" because it is a plausible example of Harry thinking like a 16 year old.

POINTS TO PONDER: "The book had become a kind of guide and friend" ... indeed, creates a sort of shadow friendship between Snape and Harry, very interesting psychologically.

WHY I LOVE JKR: This chapter is amazing ... full of ups and downs for Harry, events that are startling, dismaying, and joyous.

UNFORGETTABLE MOMENTS:

- Harry realizing the cathedral size of the Room of Requirements.
- When Ginny jumps in on Harry's behalf and points out to Hermione that Malfoy was about to do an Unforgivable curse – "you should be glad that Harry had something up his sleeve."

- The moment when Ginny and Hermione, normally so friendly, start arguing with each other over Harry is priceless. "Oh, don't start acting as though you understand Quidditch, you'll only embarrass yourself."

- Absolutely loved the moment when Ginny ran towards Harry with "a hard, blazing" look on her face. I love intense women! (Reader, I married one. ..)

Chapter 25 The Seer Overheard

SMART-ALEC SUMMARY: Harry learns (again) that Snape is a bad guy, but Dumbledore distracts him by taking him off on a Secret Mission™.

POINTS TO PONDER: I enjoyed the reference to Ron's "Pygmy Puff."

POINTS TO PONDER: Again to Slughorn's credit that he approved of Ginny. I hope Slughorn gets to do something really useful in book seven. I'd like to see this potentially very likeable character given enough "ammo" to become a friend of Harry and fan favorite.

POINTS TO PONDER: Eileen Prince is Captain of the Hogwarts Gobstones team. Gobstones is explained in *Prisoner of Azkaban* as "a wizarding game rather like marbles, in which the stones squirted a nasty-smelling liquid into other player's face when they lost a point".

POINTS TO PONDER: Liked that Harry knew that the Prince was not a girl – "I can just tell." This reinforces the theme of "shadow friendship" that Rowling has cleverly developed.

POINTS TO PONDER: Trelawney trying to hide sherry in the Room of Requirement is surprised that some students know of it ... but it's not really much of a secret, is it? They might as well give a tour on orientation day.

Ard Rhi provided a helpful check on my tendency to exaggerate:

> It *is* a secret, though. Even Dumbledore wasn't entirely clear on it when he mentioned it at the Yule Ball. The Marauders were unaware of it during their time.

POINTS TO PONDER: The big reveal occurs here as Trelawney mentions that she was "rudely interrupted by Severus Snape" the day of her interview with Dumbledore.

This is a partial payoff for all the Trelawney setup scenes earlier in the book.

Note first that Harry could have obtained this info at any time by buttering up Trelawney and asking her about her first job interview at Hogwarts ... but JKR has prudently given him an antipathy to her.

POINTS TO PONDER: Who exactly was the voice that is speaking through Trelawney? It's hinted that Trelawney has inherited a smidgeon of genuine gift from her famous ancestor, but that's begging the question ... if in the Potterverse there are occasional genuine prophecies, where do they get their 411? There are no gods, demi- or other, just a whole lot of magic floating around ... is it possible that the magic connects with itself somehow and finds a human outlet? What's its agenda? Why offer this particular prophecy?

POINTS TO PONDER: Harry zooms to Dumbledore and demands an explanation. Dumbledore sticks to the position that Snape had no way of knowing that the parents in the prophecy were people Snape knew, and Dumbledore reserves to himself once again just why he Is sure he can trust Snape completely.

POINTS TO PONDER: What could Snape *possibly* have told Dumbledore that was more convincing than "I had a change of heart"? Possibilities:

- "I'm Lily."

- "I'm pregnant by James."

- "I really, really don't like Voldemort anymore."

Gjw seems to be on the right track:

> My bet is that there was some sort of physical, convincing evidence of Snape's remorse (over betraying the Potters), such as a Pensieve memory or other mind-reading trick. In addition to the simple fact that Snape had come to him and betrayed Voldemort's most important secret (that he had to kill Harry in order to survive). Surely, even if Snape were loyal to Voldemort, that revelation would have been far beyond the bounds of what Voldemort would have allowed as part of Snape's cover. Snape, IMO, desperately wanted to save Lily. Dumbledore recognized the truth in that, and became convinced of his sincerity, but failed to see the lie about Snape's more general loyalties.

POINTS TO PONDER: Voldemort wants his favorite followers to make Horcruxes themselves and split their own souls into pieces. Actually, this is sort of plausible – Snape would not trust the idea of splitting apart his own highly protected soul.

POINTS TO PONDER: The bit at the end where Harry gives Hermione and Ron the task of watching Malfoy and Snape made me think of "General Potter." He's quite good at telling people what to do in a crisis!

It's typically admirable that Harry gives the Felix to Ron, Hermione and Ginny.

WHY I LOVE JKR: I particularly enjoyed the section of this chapter where Dumbledore closes the typical "action hero" loopholes by saying "you must follow even such orders as 'run', 'hide,' or 'go back.' Adds nicely to the characterization of Dumbledore that he delivers this line with such self-awareness and irony.

UNFORGETTABLE MOMENTS:

- The image of Harry "silently reliving a particularly happy image he had spent down at the lake with Ginny at lunchtime."

Chapter 26 The Cave

SMART-ALEC SUMMARY: What a day for a day trip …

POINTS TO PONDER: We learn that Tom Riddle climbed down the shoreside cliffs by magic. So we know he had early mastery of telekinesis.

Gjw had an interesting comment:

> It's interesting that with all of the various types of magic, JKR has shied away from actual flight (unless supported by brooms, beasts, etc.) I don't think we've even seen a scene in which a wizard is allowed to jump off a cliff and float slowly and safely to the ground... But a variant on that "Levicorpus" spell might do the trick for mountain climbing.

Dumbledore suddenly begins swimming with the agility of a much younger man – magic, or good health? Must be magic, because one of his arms is blackened and crippled by Marvolo's cursed ring.

POINTS TO PONDER: Tolkien's "Say 'friend' and enter" becomes "pay blood and enter." Advantage JRR.

POINTS TO PONDER: Dumbledore says "your blood is more valuable than mine." Why exactly? Jim McCauley wondered the same thing.

> Yup—the blood thing again. My guess is that in the ultimate encounter, Harry is going to be wounded at least as seriously as he was in the battle with the basilisk in CoS, so that his blood is available to do something unpleasantly terminal, possibly unwittingly self-inflicted, to LV. Hope Fawkes and Madame Pomfrey stay handy.

> Incidentally, I've wondered if it was Harry's blood on the serpent's fang, rather than its venom, that destroyed Riddle's diary. In CoS, JKR does write, "The basilisk venom had burned a sizzling hole right through it," but still I wonder. If Harry's blood will be required to destroy each Horcrux, he'd better start autologous donations to a blood bank right now.

Here again Dumbledore sticks with his overall strategic appreciation that Harry Potter is the single most valuable asset available to The Good Guys™. Why? The implication seems to be that he is the best chance of defeating Voldemort. The flip side of that is rather grim, namely that without Harry, The Good Guys, even with Dumbledore, don't really have a chance of defeating Voldemort.

POINTS TO PONDER: "We couldn't just try a Summoning Charm?" Harry, once more demonstrates his mastery of "Accio." I feel sure that the deciding moment in the Final Confrontation will be decided by one of Harry's "Accio" spells.

POINTS TO PONDER: Dumbledore can detect the traces of magic, even decades-old magic left by a supremely skilled wizard. We've never seen Harry do anything remotely like that. He seems to be operating with several orders of magnitude more skill than Harry can even conceive of.

POINTS TO PONDER: Dumbledore doubts that Harry's magical capacity will even register on Voldemort's detection spell because the old Voldemort is underestimating the powers of a young wizard. This even though Riddle himself was a famous child prodigy who was proficient enough as an underage wizard to make a unique and highly dangerous Horcrux diary! That a) doesn't entirely make sense and b) suggests that Riddle's skill has increased hugely since he left Hogwarts. Yet Another Scary Thought™.

POINTS TO PONDER: Harry is hard enough to do what Dumbledore asks and force him to drink the potion. He is perhaps even harder than Dumbledore.

Joe Curven and Louis Epstein exchanged an interesting pair of opposing views on this subject:

> (Curven) In this one area - emotional toughness - Harry is in fact stronger than DD.
>
> (Epstein) Honestly...I think that this is a case of Harry agreeing to follow Dumbledore's instructions and then doing so despite the instructions being a catastrophic blunder. There is simply NO excuse, the way the scene was written, for not trying to pour the potion out on the ground once it has been established that not only can the potion be "scooped up", which Dumbledore had declared it couldn't be, it can be scooped up by someone (Harry) who has NO intention of drinking it.

POINTS TO PONDER: We see the pay-off of the Inferi setups earlier in the book. Harry doesn't have much presence of mind in dealing with these animated corpses, but once roused Dumbledore is more than equal to the task.

POINTS TO PONDER: This ring of fire scene is the cover of the English book. As many of us thought when the US and UK covers were released, the English cover is much better looking, and it is a better reflection of the contents of the book.

POINTS TO PONDER: Dumbledore's technical verdict on the workmanship of Voldemort's spell: "in the end the protection was well-designed. One alone could not have done it…" In other words, given the advantages of a preset situation, Voldemort's skill was sufficient to defeat Dumbledore.

POINTS TO PONDER: This chapter is a tour-de-force set piece—for the *author*. For the *characters*, not such a great experience! Jim McCauley has a good "macro" perspective:

> This is an extremely bizarre episode. If JKR was merely writing for horror effect, she achieved it here—but really, to what end?
>
> If I may be allowed to comment of a revelation in a future chapter: Dumbledore and Harry go through all this and apparently fail to recover a real Horcrux. As I said, bizarre. Among other things, this would mean that Dd--the world's most capable wizard--was unable to detect that the hidden object was *not* a Horcrux, and he then proceeds to poison himself (involving Harry in the wretched process) in order to retrieve something that is not what they were seeking.
>
> There's an "all for nought" feel about this that, in retrospect, persuades one to speculate that there is more going on here than is literally presented. It's rather like what happened after President Kennedy was assassinated—many people were unwilling to accept that only a "lone gunman" was involved, and conspiracy theories sprouted like weeds.

UNFORGETTABLE MOMENTS:

- The effect of the potion that Dumbledore drinks is terrifying ... "It's all my fault... please make it stop." I felt like I was going to throw up first time I read this. It's horrible to see Dumbledore so vulnerable and filled with such uncharacteristic self-loathing. Indeed, this was too much for some readers, such as gjw:

    > It is a disgusting scene, and I was honestly angry with Rowling including it in a children's book. Killing a character swiftly (like she did Sirius or Cedric) is one thing. Torturing beloved characters in ghastly fashion is another.

WHY I LOVE JKR: In my view, JKR delivers the goods here ... things we never would have expected to see that are profoundly moving.

Chapter 27 The Lightning-Struck Tower

Smart-Alec summary: Bad, bad news.

Points to Ponder: At the scene with Madam Rosmerta, Harry demonstrates his "Accio" prowess with Rosmerta's brooms.

Points to Ponder: We learn later in the chapter that Rosmerta is under the Imperius Curse. I must say that this completely fooled me as it did Harry and Dumbledore. She seemed genuinely distressed. I wonder exactly what Malfoy's orders to her were?

Points to Ponder: Dumbledore lets down the spells around Hogwarts so that they can enter at speed. We know from the preceding chapter that it is possible for a great wizard to make spells that can only be undone with great investment of time and effort. So Dumbledore must have made the spells around Hogwarts of such a nature that he could always take them down quickly. Could he have provided better security with more cumbersome spells?

Perhaps, but tighter security would not have prevented the attack on Hogwarts via the Vanishing Cabinet, because Dumbledore clearly never. Interesting nonetheless to see that even high wizards encounter the fundamental tension between security and usability. (See http://www.wfzimmerman.com/2005/09/oreillys-security-and-usability-first.html).

Points to Ponder: Why exactly did Dumbledore immobilize Harry when he heard footsteps at the door? Why was that a priority over defending himself? Especially given that there were two brooms in the room and anyone entering would deduce immediately that another wizard must be present?

Jim McCauley commented:

> Draco does seem to forget the two brooms with convenient alacrity, and the four Death Eaters and Snape apparently take no notice of them at all.

Wouldn't it have been better, tactically, to fight? Is Harry really that much of a loose cannon? This decision of Dumbledore's to immobilize Harry is not explained completely to my satisfaction ... it leaves room to wonder if Dumbledore for some reason set up the whole situation with himself apparently helpless.

Zgirnius had a nice psychological and pedagogical explanation:

> The explanation I like for this action is that Dumbledore knew who was coming. That it was Draco, and he was alone. I believe that the conversation he had with Draco would have

```
been completely impossible  with a non-immobilized Harry. Harry
*would* have said something or done  something when Draco
appeared, and even if he had then shut up it would  have
changed the dynamic completely. Draco would need to keep up
appearances for his own pride far more if he *saw* Harry
standing there  looking at him.
```

POINTS TO PONDER: Interesting that Dumbledore seemingly not impressed by Malfoy's revelation that Snape was a double agent "wanting a bit of the action."

POINTS TO PONDER: Dumbledore "I appreciate the difficulty of your position." Both Katie Bell and Ron almost died as a result of Dumbledore's considerate inaction. Is this really defensible?

Ard Rhi explained it well:

```
    Dumbledore was in an untenable position. Exposing Draco
would cost dearly; Draco and possibly Narcissa would pay.
Interrogating Draco would likely  have cost Severus his
"cover". So Dumbledore had to wait, see, and hope.  Anything
else would bring consequences down on others who probably
couldn't  handle them.
```

POINTS TO PONDER: I don't really understand what Dumbledore means when he says "no, Draco, it is my mercy, and not yours, that matters now." Is Dumbledore truly helpless? Against Malfoy? Against Snape? It certainly seems possible that Dumbledore could do a non-verbal spell that would vanquish a mere Malfoy, but that he knows that nothing he can do in his present condition will beat Snape.

POINTS TO PONDER: "Severus ... please ..." JKR certainly leaves it open as to exactly what Dumbledore is pleading for. Death, or mercy?

Gjw's interpretation is "mercy" under the premise "Snape is a bad guy"?

```
    Under normal circumstances, when a person in desperate
trouble says  "please...", they are asking for assistance. (It
would be bizarre to  hear someone say that to you and then
assume that they were asking to  be murdered.)  Dumbledore had
bet his entire plan on the  trustworthiness of Snape.  Snape
would be the one to cure him when he  came back from the
Cave... Snape would be the one to rescue him &Harry from the
DE's... and then Snape appears and shatters that trust.
```

POINTS TO PONDER: "There was revulsion and hatred etched in the harsh lines of [Snape's] face" as he prepared to kill Dumbledore. Ok, revulsion and hatred directed at whom? Could still be revulsion at the idea of killing Dumbledore and hatred for either Dumbledore or Voldemort. Gjw was skeptical:

```
    The revulsion could be for a number of things (such as the
dishonorable position of having to murder a helpless old man,
or  conversely, a distaste for Dumbledore's foolish faith,
which had  brought him to this humiliating end), but I can't
imagine the hatred  being directed at anyone other than
```

> Dumbledore. You can be repulsed by a situation, but hatred is
> usually personal.

WHY I LOVE JKR: *Another* chapter that is both enigmatic and unbearably tragic

UNFORGETTABLE MOMENTS:

- The scene between Dumbledore and Malfoy is one of the best things in the whole series.
  - o "Draco, Draco, you are not a killer."
  - o "Malfoy, bizarrely, seemed to draw courage and comfort from Dumbledore's praise..."
- "Avada Kevadra!" And the rest is silence.

Chapter 28 Flight of the Prince

SMART-ALEC SUMMARY: Harry chases Snape.

POINTS TO PONDER: Harry stumbles into the free for all and fights up a storm. Ginny dodging hexes nimbly with the aid of Felix.

POINTS TO PONDER: I felt a surge of love for Neville as Harry came across him clutching his stomach but saying "I'm all right."

POINTS TO PONDER: Does JKR ever identify the "big blond" Death Eater? She must have had a compelling reason for keeping his identity secret as it becomes quite tiresome to *read* "big blond DE" over and over again, let alone type it. It would have been easy enough to have one of the side characters (McGonagall) recognize this person.

POINTS TO PONDER: Harry uses Crucio on Snape twice. Interesting that Snape tells Harry that he, Harry, doesn't have the nerve or the ability to use the Unforgivable spell. Rowling doesn't tell us or show us that Harry is in any way holding back, but Snape seems to think so, or at least to enjoy saying so. Gjw:

> Regardless of what side he is on, Severus enjoys needling Harry. Rowling HAS indicated that despite Harry not holding back, he is not up to par with some stronger wizards, though. Dumbledore had to remind Harry that love, not magic, was his weapon of choice against Voldemort. Bellatrix, Severus, and Barty Crouch Jr. have told Potter that it takes great power to use an unforgivable curse, Dumbledore again reminds Harry that his power is minimal as an unqualified wizard. The obvious implication: Harry can't rely on those powers. His trying is pointless.
>
> What I find most interesting is how others such as Umbridge and Draco manage to grasp these powers and others rather easily. I never believed Draco to be a slouch, but book six really shows him off proper. Even if he didn't pull off the Imperius or the protean, he still showed ingenuity and proper basics to get as far as he did.

POINTS TO PONDER: "Fight back! Fight back, you coward!" One of many lines that is pretty suspicious if you fall in the "Snape-is-secretly-good" camp.

POINTS TO PONDER: "Blocked again and again until you learn to keep your mouth shut and your mind closed, Potter!" Another line that sounds suspiciously like Snape is "coaching" Harry.

Blon Fel Fotch Passameer-Day Slitheen added:

> Yes, and for those who pointed out how Snape was actually
> saving Harry in this scene, (even trying to instruct him); I
> would add that he also kept Flitwick, Hermione and Luna safe
> from the deadly battle, by stupefying his colleague then
> tricking the girls into helping him. It also looks quite
> likely that Snape then saved Ginny from the huge Death Eater's
> jinx.

POINTS TO PONDER: Snape intervenes to protect Harry – "he belongs to the Dark Lord!"

A few moments later, Harry sees Snape's face "full of rage." The reason for the rage is not specified. It *could* be because of the threat to Harry.

POINTS TO PONDER: When Harry actually makes some progress and slows Snape down, Snape screams "No, Potter!" very much as if he is reprimanding someone who is actually on the same side as he is.

POINTS TO PONDER: "DON'T CALL ME COWARD!" Ok, I'll bite. Why does Snape have an issue about being called a coward? We haven't actually seen him do anything cowardly in any of the books, have we? I recall him being bullied a lot, casting nasty spells, casting nasty looks ... but never running away from a confrontation. In fact, many would argue that playing a cool double or triple game between Voldemort and Dumbledore calls for cold-blooded bravery in the most Slytherin sense. And it's not as if Slytherins particularly value bravery – that's Gryffindors – Slytherins don't put highest value on bravery. So why does it cheese Snape so much to be accused of cowardice? I know that's a fairly typical "issue" for insecure men and for mustachio-twirling villains in drama, but something just doesn't quite fit here. There must be an actual episode of painful and humiliating cowardice (or bravery) that we haven't seen yet.

Jim McCauley explained it this way:

> Harry calls Snape a coward *twice*. The first time (top of
> US page 603), Snape seems to shrug it off with a sneer and a
> jibe at Harry's father. But the second time, he's genuinely
> enraged. Why? Because by saying "Kill me like you killed him
> [Dumbledore]," Harry is calling Snape a coward for the one act
> in Snape's life that had taken the most courage—killing Dd to
> save the fight against LV. After all, it is at this point
> (paragraph 6, US page 604) that JKR writes, "[Snape's] face
> was suddenly demented, inhuman, as though he was in as much
> pain as the howling dog stuck in the burning house behind
> them"—clear evidence that Snape killed Dumbledore because he
> was trapped by fate to do so. He is raging against fate.

POINTS TO PONDER: It was a touching moment when Harry told Hagrid to use the very basic spell "Aguamenti!" to put out the fire on his house. In a way, Harry has replaced Dumbledore as Hagrid's guardian.

POINTS TO PONDER: Harry knows that the Body-Bind curse lifted only because its caster was dead. This feels very loophole-resistant.

POINTS TO PONDER: "There was still no preparation for seeing him here, spread-eagled, broken; the greatest wizard Harry had ever, or would ever, meet." A sentence that has, or will have, a fatal flaw in its construction.

POINTS TO PONDER: Not only is the Horcrux gone, but it's not Slytherin's locket – so who has it? My money's on Snape. My copy editor thinks it's at 12 Grimmauld Place.

POINTS TO PONDER: The enigmatic author of the note in the locket, "R. A. B.", does sound a lot like Regulus Black – but we can't be sure.

WHY I LOVE JKR: It's incredible that this "pursuit" scene can be read in so many enigmatic and mutually contradictory ways.

UNFORGETTABLE MOMENTS: Looking back, the thing that really stands out in my memory of this chapter is Harry's relentless pursuit of a wizard whom he knows to be his technical superior. One can imagine a sense of slowly growing confusion and fear in Snape's mind as he starts to wonder, "What sort of enemy have I created?" For although Harry is not especially skilled, he is lucky, he is ruthless, and he is absolutely determined.

Chapter 29 The Phoenix Lament

SMART-ALEC SUMMARY: Everyone's bumming.

POINTS TO PONDER: Only Ginny is able to pull Harry away from Dumbledore's body.

POINTS TO PONDER: The scene with the remnants of Dumbledore's Army at the hospital is very touching. The elegiac mood reminded me somehow of "Return of the King" after Frodo destroys the ring (except, yes, they won in ROTK).

POINTS TO PONDER: The titled "Phoenix Lament", or song of the Phoenix begins when Harry is narrating the story of Dumbledore's death and, we sense, giving way to his grief for the first time. In this and many other ways in the remaining two chapters I believe it is signaled that Harry is somehow specially connected to the Phoenix now.

POINTS TO PONDER: "Ginny's narrowed eyes focused on Fleur." It becomes apparent later in the chapter that Ginny was not secretly pulling for Fleur, rather, that she was preparing to apply high standards to her. Fortunately, they are not necessary.

POINTS TO PONDER: Does Lupin love Tonks? Even with an engraved invitation and the endorsement of the local wise woman (Mrs. W) he holds back.

POINTS TO PONDER: Harry's version of what Snape told Dumbledore to get in good with him is not entirely accurate.

POINTS TO PONDER: After reading a lot of people saying how much they love Fred and George Weasley, I was very disappointed to learn that their Peruvian Instant Darkness Powder was instrumental in the attack on Hogwarts. Unfortunately, Ron's pledge to "talk to them" lacked some, well, heft. I would have been happier with a pledge that if they ever sell to the Dark again he will personally feed them their guts for garters.

POINTS TO PONDER: "'Luckily,' Lupin says, his party ran into the Felix-enhanced versions of Ron and Ginny almost immediately after setting out. At this point in the discussion, Lupin has obviously not yet been clued in to the presence of Felix in the scenario..

POINTS TO PONDER: Yet another ambivalent scene where Snape stupefied Flitwick (and lets Hermione and Luna live). That was by far the most sensible thing to do; it would not have been very smart to burn bridges by killing them in response to at what very well might have been a false alarm

POINTS TO PONDER: The teachers showed their true colors in the meeting in Dumbledore's office. I was disappointed, but should not be surprised, that Slughorn wavered.

POINTS TO PONDER: We're told that the Phoenix had left Hogwarts forever … but we're not told that the Phoenix has left Harry. I think it'll be back!

WHY I LOVE JKR: The palpable sense of very real grief and mourning at Hogwarts, yet with the moments of human redemption shining through, as in Fleur's speech to Mrs. Weasley.

UNFORGETTABLE MOMENTS:

- The scene in Dumbledore's office where he is sleeping in the portrait on the wall really got me.

- Mrs. Weasley offering Fleur the use of her tiara at the wedding.

- The Fat Lady's wordless cry at the news of Dumbledore's death.

Chapter 30 The White Tomb

SMART-ALEC SUMMARY: At the beginning of the chapter, a number of characters undergo minor development.

POINTS TO PONDER: Seamus Finnegan refuses point-blank to go home – will we see slightly more of him in book seven?

POINTS TO PONDER: Madame Maxine arrives to visit Hagrid. For reasons that aren't entirely clear to me, JKR writes the scene from the point of view of underclassmen who don't know her, instead of from the point of view of the majority of Hogwarts students (and our favorite characters) who all do know her by name.

POINTS TO PONDER: Bill Weasley now bears a distinct resemblance to Mad-Eye Moody and likes raw meat. This sounds a bit ominous.

POINTS TO PONDER: Harry begins to master the complex art of having a girlfriend as he comments that Fleur is "ugly, though."

POINTS TO PONDER: Harry rehearses the plot for book seven in his head: "the locket … the cup … the snake … something of Gryffindor's or Ravenclaw's." My money is that Horcrux #4 will be something of Ravenclaw's, simply because we haven't seen enough of them yet.

POINTS TO PONDER: I liked Harry's fury at Dumbledore's "inexcusable trust in Snape", and then, even better, Harry's realization that "he, Harry, had been taken in just the same." He had refused to believe ill of the boy **who had been so clever, who had helped him so much.** JKR is showing Harry learn something that is often very difficult to learn: that people who have many admirable qualities and do many helpful things can be among those who do us the most harm.

POINTS TO PONDER: Interesting that Harry "did not look for some kind of loophole." Looks to me as if JKR is showing Harry's increasing maturity in the face of loss and grief. In this light, it seems almost inconceivable that she would allow Dumbledore to return in book seven. Dead is dead.

POINTS TO PONDER: Harry now feels "the tiniest drop of pity" for Malfoy. Compare Frodo and Gollum. Advantage: Tolkien.

POINTS TO PONDER: Madame Pince is with Filch. Hmm?? Two different takes:

```
(Kish): Ick. Ew.

(Traugott Vitz): Hey guys, who says going together to a
funeral has anything to do with romance? Madame Pince and Mr
Filch have in common that they are  members of the Hogwarts
```

```
staff, yet not members of the  TEACHING staff.  Look at
official occasions you know from the Muggle world  where all
members of the "firm" have to appear - wouldn't  you expect to
associate the "lower orders" among themselves,  and the "big
shots" to have adjacent seats?  I'd bet there's no more to the
Pince/Filch "romance"  than just that.
```

POINTS TO PONDER: The funeral: who gives the eulogy? For some reason I thought "Nicholas Flamel," but according to jkrowling.com Flamel is dead—presumably prior to *Half-Blood Prince.*

POINTS TO PONDER: Anyone missing from the funeral?

POINTS TO PONDER: The scene with the fire around Dumbledore's body and the creation of the white tomb raises many questions.

POINTS TO PONDER: Where did the magic come from? The fire, the phoenix, and the white tomb on the grounds of Hogwarts are all characteristically Dumbledorian magic. Did someone else cast the spell? Apparently not, because everyone at the funeral seems surprised. But if Dumbledore's dead, how could he cast a spell?

POINTS TO PONDER: I lean towards the view that some sort of white magic focused on love and loyalty was bound up with Dumbledore's life and that therefore the "phoenix/tomb" spell already existed – its release was triggered by the end of Dumbledore's funeral. I also suspect that this "phoenix magic" will reappear in book seven. The scene with Scrimgeour underlines that Harry is Dumbledore's true heir and thus the most likely locus for the phoenix magic. "I am Dumbledore's man through and through..." he will only be gone from the school when none here are loyal to him" (Seamus Finnegan, Luna, Neville, McGonagall, Sprout ...)

POINTS TO PONDER: Great moment when Harry realizes there will be no more protectors, and that indeed, he must be the protector now (of Ginny). As Ard Rhi commented, a bit sarcastically,

```
Spider-Man would be proud.
```

("With great power comes great responsibility...")

POINTS TO PONDER: The whole Ginny break-up thing didn't make much sense to me, at least in terms of the reasons Harry gives (and Ginny accepts).

Helena Bowles had a nice three-dimensional take on this:

```
     I think that this scene should be considered in the light of
what  happened between Lupin and Tonks. Effectively what Lupin
seems to have said  to Tonks is analogous to what Harry says to
Ginny: "I'm too dangerous to be  around." (Okay in Lupin's case
he's bolstering his argument with "old" - I'm  insulted, he's
the same age as me! ;-)  and "poor"). Lupin, through  self-
sacrifice and nobility, has merely made Tonks thoroughly
miserable. In  both Lupin and Harry's cases they are not brave
```

enough to allow the women in their lives to take their own
risks because *Lupin and Harry* cannot bear to think of their
own pain if something goes wrong... and in both cases they
are limiting their own happiness (which probably makes both of
them feel disgustingly noble!)

So what can we take from Tonks and Ginny's reactions? Well
Tonks is either not as clever as Ginny - or, more likely, more
desperate! Ginny has grown up with six brothers. She probably
understands enough of male psychology to know that a direct
attack on Harry's assumptions won't work... and a funeral is
hardly the appropriate place to cause a scene. Whilst both
Harry and Lupin are scarred by multiple losses and are marked
out as something different and isolated - Lupin by his
lycanthropy and Harry as the "Chosen One" Harry, being younger
and more open than Lupin (who seems in the books to be an
intensely private person so Tonks must *really* have been
desperate to approach him in *public*) probably won't be able
to hold out as long as Lupin seems to have. Although he is
very stubborn so...

We also have the Fleur/Bill comparison - directly with
Lupin/Tonks, indirectly with Harry/Ginny which serves to show
Lupin that Tonks is not alone in loyalty to a man who is not
perfect and suggests to the reader that in times like this
happiness should be seized where it can be.

I very much doubt Ginny has given up on Harry... she's a lot
more dynamic a character than that.

POINTS TO PONDER: Surely Voldemort knows that Ginny and Harry are an item by now. Zoltan47 put his finger on the problem:

What, Voldemort is going to say, "So, Harry Potter has
himself a girlfriend. Just what I need to cause him even more
pain. What? They've broken up? Oh bugger! Well, never mind."

POINTS TO PONDER: According to the trio confab at the end of the book, the agenda for the first part of book seven is:

- Dursleys

- Bill and Fleur's wedding

- Godric's Hollow

- The hunt for the Horcruxes.

WHY I LOVE JKR: So much is resolved in this book, yet so much is left open.

UNFORGETTABLE MOMENTS:

- The white tomb.

- Fawkes.

- Ron and Hermione telling Harry they will be with him to the end.

What we expected for book six

Prior to the release of *Harry Potter and the Half-Blood Prince*, J. K. Rowling made a variety of comments as to things that might be in books six or seven. In the following sections I will analyze what she said <u>before</u> *Half-Blood Prince* versus what we actually got in *Half-Blood Prince*. I will also try to identify what is "left over" that has been promised for books six or seven but has not yet occurred, and that we may therefore expect to see in book seven.

What we expected: More on the war between Voldemort and the good guys.

> "In the fifth and most recent book, Harry Potter and the Order of the Phoenix, the last chapter, titled "The Second War Begins," started:
>
> 'In a brief statement Friday night, Minister of Magic Cornelius Fudge confirmed that He-Who-Must-Not-Be-Named has returned to this country and is active once more.
>
> "It is with great regret that I must confirm that the wizard styling himself Lord - well, you know who I mean - is alive among us again," said Fudge.'
>
> Harry Potter and the Half-Blood Prince takes up the story of Harry Potter's sixth year at Hogwarts School of Witchcraft and Wizardry at this point in the midst of the storm of this battle of good and evil."(Scholastic press release, December 21, 2004; http://www.scholastic.com/aboutscholastic/news/press_122104.htm).

What we got:

Fudge disappeared at the end of the first chapter and was scarcely seen again. Remarkably, Voldemort was off-stage for the entirety of book six. And we saw very little of the war ... only the "campaign for Hogwarts," which mainly consisted of reconnaissance and feints by Malfoy and Harry.

What we expected: Harry makes a short stay at 4 Privet Drive.

> Adele: Will poor Harry be stuck at the Dursleys' all next summer?
>
> JK Rowling replies -> Not all summer, no. In fact, he has the shortest stay in Privet Drive so far. (World Book Day chat, 3/04/04, http://www.mugglenet.com/jkrwbd.shtml).

What we got:

It was indeed a short stay ... but one of the most memorable ones as Dumbledore delivers the ticking off of a lifetime to the Dursleys.

A pleasant escape from 4 Privet Drive.

> The theory that [Harry stands trial again in HP&THBP] has been put forward to explain why Harry does not spend as long in Privet Drive during this book as previous ones, but I am happy to say that he leaves the Dursleys early for a much pleasanter reason than a court case.
>
> (http://www.jkrowling.com/textonly/rumours_view.cfm?id=23)

What we got:

The trip to Slughorn's was not exactly pleasant, but the subsequent trip to the Weasleys was.

What we expected: An update (and probably some major plot action) on Peter Pettigrew.

> Rita: What about Wormtail? Is there hope for redemption?
>
> JK Rowling replies -> There's always hope, of course. You'll find out more about our rat-like friend in book six. (World Book Day chat, 3/04/04, http://www.mugglenet.com/jkrwbd.shtml).

What we got:

Actually, very little about Pettigrew: He's living with Snape.

What we expected: more about Harry's love life, and a little less random anger.

> polly weasley: Will Harry fall for another girl in book six, or will he be too busy for romance?
>
> JK Rowling replies -> He'll be busy, but what's life without a little romance? In book six, the wizarding world is really at war again and he has to master his own feelings to make himself useful. (World Book Day chat, 3/04/04, http://www.mugglenet.com/jkrwbd.shtml).

What we got:

A full-fledged romance with Ginny. And yes, much of Harry's activities in book six involve mastering his own feelings to make himself useful. He spends the middle two-thirds of the book struggling with the monster that is his jealousy towards Dean and Ginny. (In case you're wondering how there can be a middle two-thirds of anything, that's one sixth, two-thirds, one-sixth.)

More about Hagrid's half-brother Grawp.

> Kings Park primary school: What will happen to Hagrid's half brother?
>
> JK Rowling replies -> you'll find out in book six. Luckily he's become a little more controllable. (World Book Day, http://www.mugglenet.com/jkrwbd.shtml ,3/4/04).
>
> Will Hagrid ever succeed with his plans for his brother?
>
> In a limited way, yes. Grawp is obviously the very stupidest thing that Hagrid ever brought home. In his long line of bringing home stupid things—Aragog, the Blast-Ended Skrewts— Grawp is the one that should have finished him off, but ironically it might be the one time that a monstrous something came good. By the next book, Grawp is a little bit more controllable. I think you got a clue to that at the end of Phoenix, because Grawp was starting to speak and to be a little bit more amenable to human contact. (Edinburgh Book Festival, 8/15/04, http://www.jkrowling.com/textonly/news_view.cfm?id=80)

What we got:

At the very end of the book, at Dumbledore's funeral in chapter 30, there is a very affecting sequence where Grawp cares for the bereaved Hagrid.

What we expected: more magical activity in Muggledom.

> Calliope: Are the Muggle and Magical worlds ever going to be rejoined?
>
> JK Rowling replies -> No, the breach was final, although as book six shows, the Muggles are noticing more and more odd happenings now that Voldemort's back. (World Book Day chat, 3/04/04, http://www.mugglenet.com/jkrwbd.shtml).

What we got:

A few headlines in The Daily Prophet, and Arthur Weasley appointed to a new position at the Ministry.

What we expected: more about Voldemort's origins.

> mnich: Was Voldemort born evil?
>
> JK Rowling replies -> I don't believe that anybody was born evil. You will find out more about the circumstances of his birth in the next book. (World Book Day chat, 04/04/2004, http://www.mugglenet.com/jkrwbd.shtml).

What we got:

This is rather an interesting one. From the evidence that JKR presents in book six, it seems that Riddle became evil sometime after birth but well before Dumbledore picked him up. At least, JKR seems to indicate that while Miss Cole and the others at the orphanage may not have been ideal foster parents, they were not extravagantly abusive, and there were plenty of orphans in the same situation who grew up without Riddle's need for power, control, and domination.

What we expected: something about the Hogwarts Graveyard.

Question: What was it like meeting JK, what was her advice like?

> Alfonso: She [Rowling] said I should stay faithful to the spirit of the book not literal. That was entrusting me a lot of freedom. But freedom and responsibility is the same thing - I was like 'oh gosh - am I being faithful to the spirit?'
>
> The amazing thing with JK as a collaborator is she doesn't stop you doing anything. The way she approaches it has nothing to do with 'I like' or 'I dislike' it's 'this makes sense' or 'it doesn't make sense in this universe.'
>
> I give you an example: There's a scene where Malfoy wants to see Buckbeak being executed. It's where Hermione punches him. And there's a sundial. We thought we need something there. I said 'Let's put a graveyard there'.

```
She says: 'No, you can't have a graveyard there'. And I'm like,
'Why?' She says: 'Oh because the graveyard is near this other
wing of the castle and it's going to play an important part in
number six because such and such and such. (CBBC Newsround,
5/28/04,,
http://news.bbc.co.uk/cbbcnews/hi/tv_film/newsid_3758000/375810
1.stm)
```

Kudos to the sharp-eyed guys at http://www.halfbloodprince.info for spotting this one, referenced in an interview with "Azkaban" director Alfonso Cuaron.

What we got:

I'm not sure I understand what JKR was talking about in this comment. The first thing that comes to mind is The White Tomb where Dumbledore is buried.

What we expected: more of Moaning Myrtle.

```
    novell: I find moaning myrtle is the saddest character in
your books, inspiring a mixture of revulsion and pity. Does she
play any further part?

    JK Rowling replies -> You do see her again. Don't you like
her? I know she's a bit revolting, but that's why I'm so fond
of her. (World Book Day chat, 3/04/04,
http://www.mugglenet.com/jkrwbd.shtml).
```

Summary of what we expected/what we got:

Everything that was promised was delivered. But the sum total of these comments represents only a very thin slice of the content of book six. The moral: what JKR says in public about book seven before publication will leave out most of what makes it great!

What We Know about Harry Potter Book Seven

This chapter summarizes and discusses public statements by J. K. Rowling and others about the contents of Harry Potter book seven.

Finally ... book seven!

After "Harry Potter and the Half-Blood Prince" will come Harry Potter book seven, the culmination of the series.

- No one knows yet what the title will be—but there is a set of plausible candidates.

- No one knows yet when the book will come out—but it will probably be within a year or two of publication of HBP.

- No-one knows everything that the book will contain— but J. K. Rowling has dropped a lot of hints over the years about what will, won't, and may be found in book seven.

How long will book seven be?

Chances are that it will be shorter than "Order of the Phoenix," the heavyweight champ of the series, as Rowling has said she does not want to keep churning out "baby hippos." (jkrowling.com, http://www.jkrowling.com/textonly/faq_view.cfm?id=35) My own guess is that it will be quite a bit shorter, more like the length of "Chamber of Secrets" or "Azkaban." Rowling knows what has to be in book seven, and she will take as much space as it needs, no more, no less. ✗

Things we will now definitely see in book seven

There are a lot of important things that we know for sure we will find out in Harry Potter book seven.

THE ANSWER TO THE "TWO QUESTIONS"

One of the very most important clues that J. K. Rowling has ever offered to the mystery underlying the end of the series came near the end of her chat at the Edinburgh Book Festival in August 2004.

> I thought that I would give you something though, rather than get to the end of today and think that I have not given you a lot. There are two questions that I have never been asked but that I should have been asked, if you know what I mean. If you want to speculate on anything, you should speculate on these two things, which will point you in the right direction.
>
> The first question that I have never been asked—it has probably been asked in a chatroom but no one has ever asked me—is, "Why didn't Voldemort die?" Not, "Why did Harry live?" but, "Why didn't Voldemort die?" The killing curse rebounded, so he should have died. Why didn't he?
>
> At the end of Goblet of Fire he says that one or more of the steps that he took enabled him to survive. You should be wondering what he did to make sure that he did not die—I will put it that way. I don't think that it is guessable. It may be—someone could guess it—but you should be asking yourself that question, particularly now that you know about the prophesy. I'd better stop there or I will really incriminate myself.
>
> The other question that I am surprised no one has asked me since Phoenix came out—I thought that people would—is why Dumbledore did not kill or try to kill Voldemort in the scene in the ministry. I know that I am giving a lot away to people who have not read the book. Although Dumbledore gives a kind of reason to Voldemort, it is not the real reason.
>
> When I mentioned that question to my husband—I told Neil that I was going to mention it to you—he said that it was because Voldemort knows that there are two more books to come. As you can see, we are on the same literary wavelength. [Laughter]. That is not the answer; Dumbledore knows something slightly more profound than that. If you want to wonder about anything, I would advise you to concentrate on those two questions. That might take you a little bit further. (Edinburgh Book Festival, 8/15/2004, http://www.jkrowling.com/textonly/news_view.cfm?id=80) ✗

MORE ABOUT HARRY

Rowling has dropped various tidbits about things pertaining to Harry Potter's person. For example, **his scar:**

> Cathedral: Don't want to ruin the ending, but will we be finding out more about the significance of the shape of Harry's scar in future books?
>
> JK Rowling: The shape is not the most significant aspect of that scar, and that's all I'm going to say! ! (World Book Day chat, 3/4/04, http://www.wizardnews.com/story.200403042.html)

More about the scar.

> In plotting Harry's journey she has already completed a draft of the final chapter of the last book. "I constantly rewrite," she says. "At the moment, the last word is 'scar." (People Magazine, 12/31/99, reproduced at http://www.quick-quote-quill.org/articles/1999/1299-people.html).

And the color of his eyes:

> Sussie: Does Harry's eye colour become important in the future books, like we've heard?
>
> JK Rowling replies -> No comment! ! (World Book Day chat, 3/4/04, http://www.wizardnews.com/story.200403042.html)

Early in every book, there is a description of Harry's green eyes.

The explanation of why James Potter died before Lily Potter.

> At the end of 'Goblet of Fire', in which order should Harry's parents have come out of the wand?
>
> Lily first, then James. That's how it appears in my original manuscript but we were under enormous pressure to edit it very fast and my American editor thought that was the wrong way around, and he is so good at catching small errors I changed it without thinking, then realised it had been right in the first place. We were all very sleep-deprived at the time.

Something "incredibly important" about Harry Potter's mother.

> Now, the - the important thing about Harry's mother - the really, really significant thing - you're going to find out in two - in two parts. You'll find out a lot more about her in book five, or you'll find out something very significant about her in book five, and you'll find out something incredibly important about her in book seven. . ("The Connection" radio show, 10/12/99, http://www.hogwarts-

library.net/reference/interviews/19991012_TheConnection.txt).

MORE ABOUT SNAPE, AND LESS ABOUT BAD BOYS …

J. K. Rowling has promised that **we will learn more about everyone's favorite nasty teacher.**

> Also, will we see more of Snape?

> You always see a lot of Snape, because he is a gift of a character. I hesitate to say that I love him. [Audience member: I do]. You do? This is a very worrying thing. Are you thinking about Alan Rickman or about Snape? [Laughter]. Isn't this life, though? I make this hero—Harry, obviously— and there he is on the screen, the perfect Harry, because Dan is very much as I imagine Harry, but who does every girl under the age of 15 fall in love with? Tom Felton as Draco Malfoy. Girls, stop going for the bad guy. Go for a nice man in the first place. It took me 35 years to learn that, but I am giving you that nugget free, right now, at the beginning of your love lives.

And at the Edinburgh Book Festival she said:

> Apart from Harry, Snape is my favourite character because he is so complex and I just love him. Can he see the Thestrals, and if so, why? Also, is he a pure blood wizard?

> Snape's ancestry is hinted at. He was a Death Eater, so clearly he is no Muggle born, because Muggle-borns are not allowed to be Death Eaters, except in rare circumstances. You have some information about his ancestry there. He can see Thestrals, but in my imagination most of the older people at Hogwarts would be able to see them because, obviously, as you go through life you do lose people and understand what death is. But you must not forget that Snape was a Death Eater. He will have seen things that… Why do you love him? Why do people love Snape? I do not understand this. Again, it's bad boy syndrome, isn't it? It's very depressing. [Laughter]. One of my best friends watched the film and she said, "You know who's really attractive?" I said, "Who?" She said, "Lucius Malfoy!" (Edinburgh Book Festival, 8/15/04).

Something "stunning" (and probably not good) about Professor Snape.

> Lydon: Er - one of our connec- one of our internet correspondents wondered if Snape is going to fall in love?

> JKR: Yeah? Who on earth would want Snape in love with them, that is a very horrible idea. Erm ...

> Lydon: But you'd get an important kind of redemptive pattern to Snape

```
     JKR: It is, isn't it ... I got ... There's so much I
wish I could say to you, and I can't   because it'd ruin ...
I promise you ... whoever asked that question, can I just
say to you that I'm - I'm slightly stunned that you've said
that - erm - and you'll find out why I'm so stunned if you
read book 7. ("The Connection" radio show, 10/12/99,
http://www.hogwarts-
library.net/reference/interviews/19991012_TheConnection.txt
).
```

When I re-read the series after seeing this comment, I noticed something ... if
you read what J. K. Rowling actually writes, Snape never does anything nice.
Ever. The idea that he's a good guy underneath it all comes strictly from our
imaginations.

OTHER THINGS WE'LL SEE

A new Minister of Magic.

```
     Miggs: Is there going to be a new minister of magic in
the next books?

     JK Rowling: Yes. Ha! Finally, a concrete bit of
information, I hear you cry! (World Book Day chat, 3/4/04,
http://www.wizardnews.com/story.200403042.html)
```

The fate of Sirius Black's flying motorbike.

```
     Rita: Whatever happened to Sirius' flying motorbike?

     JK Rowling:, good question. You'll find out, but the
real sleuths among you might be able to guess! (World Book
Day chat, 3/4/04,
http://www.wizardnews.com/story.200403042.html)
```

The fate of Sirius's two-way mirror.

```
     Kelpie_8: Will the two way mirror Sirius gave Harry ever
show up again?

     JK Rowling: Ooooo good question. There's your answer.!
(World Book Day chat, 3/4/04,
http://www.wizardnews.com/story.200403042.html)

     Why did Harry have to forget the mirror he had been
given by Sirius in 'Order of the Phoenix'?

     I can't give a full answer to this, because it is
relevant to books six and seven. However, the short answer
is that Harry was determined never to use the mirror, as is
clearly stated in chapter 24: 'he knew he would never use
whatever it was'. For once in Harry's life, he does not
succumb to curiosity, he hides the mirror and the temptation
away from himself, and then, when it might have been useful,
he has forgotten it.
```

The mirror might not have helped as much as you think, but on the other hand, will help more than you think. You'll have to read the final books to understand that! (jkrowling.com, http://www.jkrowling.com/textonly/faq_view.cfm?id=23)

More about Tonks.

LizardLaugh: I love Tonks, she's my favorite new character. Will she play a large role in future books and/or in Harry's life? JK Rowling replies -> Tonks is hanging around. I really like her, too. ! (World Book Day chat, 3/4/04, http://www.wizardnews.com/story.200403042.html)

Nothing whatsoever about Hermione and Draco Malfoy as a couple!

Chibimono: Do you have any future plans in particular for Draco Malfoy?

JK Rowling replies -> I've got plans for all my characters. Actually, this is a really good place to answer a question about Draco and Hermione, which a certain Ms. Radcliffe is desperate to have answered. Will they end up together in book six/seven? NO! The trouble is, of course, that girls fancy Tom Felton, but Draco is NOT Tom Felton! (My daughter likes TF very much too, because he taught her how to use a diablo)

Mad Eye Moody, just as we love and remember him.

SnapesForte: Is Mad Eye Moody the real Moody this time? And if he is, is he up to something fishy? Because he's acting too much like Crouch jr - sniffing food etc.

JK Rowling replies -> It's the other way around - Crouch Jnr. acted just like the real Moody. (World Book Day chat, 3/04/04, http://www.mugglenet.com/jkrwbd.shtml).

Much less about Cho Chang.

eastbrook4: why did Harry have to split up with Cho Chang?

JK Rowling replies -> That's life, I'm afraid. They were never going to be happy, it was better that it ended early! (World Book Day chat, 3/04/04, http://www.mugglenet.com/jkrwbd.shtml).

A little about Krum.

bertieana: Will we be seeing Krum again any time soon?

JK Rowling replies -> You will see Krum again, though not soon. (World Book Day chat, 3/04/04, http://www.mugglenet.com/jkrwbd.shtml).

What makes some witches and wizards become ghosts after they die, and some not.

> You don't really find that out until Book VII, but I can say that the happiest people do not become ghosts. As you might guess, Moaning Myrtle! (Scholastic live interview, 2/3/00,
> http://www.scholastic.com/harrypotter/author/transcript1.htm

A NEAT, BUT SAD, ENDING

There will not be a lot of loose ends.

> P: Are you going to have a lot of loose ends to tie up in 7?
>
> JKR: Oh god, I hope not. I'm aiming to tie it all up neatly in a nice big knot... that's it, good night. (CBC Newsround, 6/19/03,
> http://news.bbc.co.uk/cbbcnews/hi/uk/newsid_3004000/3004878.stm) ↗

What happens to everyone.

> The final chapter for Book Seven is written. I wrote that just for my own satisfaction, really as an act of faith. (To say) I will get here in the end. In that chapter you do, I hope, feel a sense of resolution. You do find out what happens to the survivors. I know that sounds very ominous (laughs). (The Oregonian, 10/20/00, http://www.quick-quote-quill.org/articles/2000/1000-oregonian-baker.htm).

One of Harry's classmates ends up as a teacher at Hogwarts.

> JKR: Erm, well, because all your kids said hello so nicely in the background there, I'm going to give you information I haven't given anyone else, and I will tell you that one of the characters - er - one of - one of Harry's class mates, though it's not Harry himself, does end up a teacher at Hogwarts, but _it__is__not__maybe__the__one__you'd__think_ - hint, hint, hint! So, yes one of them does end up staying at Hogwarts, but - erm ...
>
> Lydon: Does the kids want to have a guess at it, Kathleen?
>
> Kathleen: Do you like to have a guess at who it is?
>
> Class: Ron
>
> Kathleen: They say Ron ...
>
> JKR: Noooo - it's not Ron ...
>
> Kathleen: [to class] it's not Ron ...

> JKR: ... because I can't see Ron as a teacher, no way. ("The Connection" radio show, 10/12/99, http://www.hogwarts-library.net/reference/interviews/19991012_TheConnection.txt [(My money's on Neville Longbottom.)

More deaths.

> Are you going to kill any more characters?

> Yes. Sorry. (jkrowling.com, http://www.jkrowling.com/textonly/faq_view.cfm?id=68)

Don't you wish you had been a fly on this wall?

Mugglenet Chatroom Uninterested in JKR's Theories

A few weeks ago I did something I've never done before and took a stroll into a Harry Potter chat room: specifically, MuggleNet's chat room. Although I was concerned to find that many of the moderators feel their spiritual home is Slytherin, this is a great site.

Nobody was remotely interested in my theories about what's going to happen in book seven, though. (jkrowling.com, http://www.jkrowling.com/textonly/news_view.cfm?id=63)

Things we will NOT see in book seven

This is a good place to refute some of the more absurd rumors that you may have encountered. As Mark Twain said, it's not the things you don't know, it's the things you think you know that ain't so. Here are a few possibilities that will *not* happen.

We will not see anyone who is definitely dead come back to life. This specifically includes Harry's mother.

> Lydon: Peter, what is your guess about Lily - the real story about Harry's mother?
>
> Peter: Er - I don't really know, but I'm guessing that maybe she is going to come back to life, maybe in the seventh book or something like that ...
>
> JKR: Well, it would be nice, but - I'll tell you something - you - you've raised a really interesting point there, Peter, because when I started writing the books, the first thing I had to decide was not what magic /can/ do, but what it /can't/ do. I had to set limits on it - immediately, and decide what the parameters are ... and one of the most important things I - I decided was that _magic__cannot__bring__dead__people__back to life; that' - that's one of the most profound things, the - the natural law of - of - of death applies to wizards as it applies to Muggles and there is no returning once you're properly dead, you know, they might be able to save very close-to-death people better than we can, by magic - that they - that they have certain knowledge we don't, but once you're dead, you're dead.
>
> So - erm - yeah, I'm afraid there will be no coming back- for Harry's parents.

Harry Potter's mother Lily as a nasty former Death Eater. In the "Rumours" section of her website, J. K. Rowling refutes the idea his way:

> How dare you?! (jkrowling.com, http://www.jkrowling.com/textonly/rumours_view.cfm?id=5).

Neville Longbottom as Peter Pettigrew's son. [Eww... gross! /wfz]

> See response for 'Lily Potter was a Death Eater' above. (jkrowling.com, http://www.jkrowling.com/textonly/rumours_view.cfm?id=8).

We will *not* see Harry become an animagus.

> Sean Bullard (NPR): We're going to take a few more questions and um, the next one is: "Will Harry ever turn into a *shape-changer* like his father?"

> J.K. Rowling: No, Harry's not in training to be an animagus. If you ... unless you've read book 3, you won't know ... that's a wizard that ... it's very, very difficult to do. They, they ... learn to turn themselves into animals. No, Harry is not ... Harry's energies are going to be concentrated elsewhere and he's not going to have time to do that. He's got quite a full agenda coming up, poor, poor boy. (National Press Club Luncheon, 10/20/99, http://www.hogwarts-library.net/reference/interviews/19991020_NPCLuncheon.html)

Harry as a relative of Voldemort.

> Is Voldemort some sort of relative of Harry's? Possibly his mother's brother?

> Rowling: I'm laughing...that would be a bit Star Wars, wouldn't it? (Scholastic live interview, 10/16/00, http://www.scholastic.com/harrypotter/author/transcript2.htm)

And, **rebutting the rumor that "Voldemort is Harry's real father/grandfather/close relative of some description,"** J. K. Rowling got pretty excited:

> No, no, no, no, no. You lot have been watching much too much Star Wars. James is DEFINITELY Harry's father. Doesn't everybody Harry meets say 'you look just like your father'? And hasn't Dumbledore already told Harry that Voldemort is the last surviving descendent of Salazar Slytherin? Just to clarify - this means that Harry is NOT a descendent of Salazar Slytherin.
> (http://www.jkrowling.com/textonly/rumours_view.cfm?id=3)

Dumbledore as Harry's grandfather.

> If Dumbledore had been Harry's grandfather, why on earth would he have been sent to live with the Dursleys? (jkrowling.com)

The long-lost love of Tom Riddle's life.

> Has Voldemort or Tom Riddle ever cared for or loved anyone?

> Now, that's a cracking question to end with—very good. No, never. [Laughter.] If he had, he couldn't possibly be what he is. You will find out a lot more about that. It is a good question, because it leads us rather neatly to Half Blood Prince, although I repeat for the millionth time that Voldemort is not the half blood prince, which is what a lot of people thought. He is definitely, definitely not.

Hermione's little brother. "Shermione."

Does Hermione have any brothers or sisters?

No, she doesn't. When I first made up Hermione I gave her a younger sister, but she was very hard to work in. The younger sister was not supposed to go to Hogwarts. She was supposed to remain a Muggle. It was a sideline that didn't work very well and it did not have a big place in the story. I have deliberately kept Hermione's family in the background. You see so much of Ron's family so I thought that I would keep Hermione's family, by contrast, quite ordinary. They are dentists, as you know. They are a bit bemused by their odd daughter but quite proud of her all the same. (Edinburgh Book Festival, 8/15/04, http://www.jkrowling.com/textonly/news_view.cfm?id=80)

Harry's mysterious (and non-existent) godmother.

Does Harry have a godmother? If so, will she make an appearance in future books?

No, he doesn't. I have thought this through. If Sirius had married... Sirius was too busy being a big rebel to get married. When Harry was born, it was at the very height of Voldemort fever last time so his christening was a very hurried, quiet affair with just Sirius, just the best friend. At that point it looked as if the Potters would have to go into hiding so obviously they could not do the big christening thing and invite lots of people. Sirius is the only one, unfortunately. I have got to be careful what I say there, haven't I? (Edinburgh Book Festival, 8/15/04, http://www.jkrowling.com/textonly/news_view.cfm?id=80).

Voldemort called "Voldie," or morphing into a good guy.

I would like to take this opportunity to say that the practise of calling Lord Voldemort 'Voldie' must stop, as must the insistence that with a bit of therapy 'Voldie' would be a real sweetheart. (jkrowling.com, http://www.jkrowling.com/textonly/news_view.cfm?id=63)

Voldemort in Tom Riddle's 16-year-old body from Chamber of Secrets.

In 'Chamber of Secrets', what would have happened if Ginny had died and Tom Riddle had escaped the diary?

I can't answer that fully until all seven books are finished, but it would have strengthened the present-day Voldemort considerably. (jkrowling.com, http://www.jkrowling.com/textonly/faq_view.cfm?id=17)

http://www.jkrowling.com/textonly/news_view.cfm?id=80).

Harry as Minister of Magic.

> Seventeen is much too young to enter politics.
> (jkrowling.com,
> http://www.jkrowling.com/textonly/rumours_view.cfm?id=12)

Nor will Arthur Weasley be the new Minister for Magic.

> "Alas, no." (jkrowling.com,
> http://www.jkrowling.com/textonly/faq_view.cfm?id=59) ⚡

"Icicle," or "Professor Bicycle."

> I have been told that I once promised a character with
> this name during an interview. I can only think that
> somebody misheard what I said because at no stage have I
> ever planned a character called 'Icicle.'
>
> Professor Bicycle, on the other hand, will be a key
> figure in books six and seven.*
>
> *this is a joke (jkrowling.com,
> http://www.jkrowling.com/textonly/rumours_view.cfm?id=1)

J.K. Rowling's patented memory-erasing device.

> You would all like me to tell you exactly what happens
> in books six and seven and then to erase your memories so
> that you can read them. I know, because that is how I feel
> about things that I really enjoy. I would kind of like to do
> it, but at the same time I know that I would ruin it for
> everyone. (Edinburgh Book Festival, 8/15/04,
> http://www.jkrowling.com/textonly/news_view.cfm?id=80). ⚡

Things we may see in book seven

The door has been left open on a few intriguing items. More will be added to this list in subsequent editions!

Ron & Hermione together

> Will Ron and Hermione ever get together?
>
> Well—[Laughter.] What do you think? [Audience member: I think they will]. I'm not going to say. I can't say, can I? I think that, by now, I've given quite a lot of clues on the subject. That is all I'm going to say. You will have to read between the lines on that one. (Edinburgh Book Festival, 8/15/04,

More about the moral and religious implications of the books.

> Rowling, aware of the protest, said she couldn't answer the questions about the book's religious content until the conclusion of book seven. (Chicago Sun-Times, 10/22/99, http://www.quick-quote-quill.org/articles/1999/1099-chictimes-tucker.html).

Invincible Voldemort?

> pablo: If Harry dies in the ending of the books, will Voldemort be invincible?
>
> JK Rowling replies -> Pablo, I can't possibly answer. You'll have to read book seven! (World Book Day Chat, 3/04/04, http://www.mugglenet.com/jkrwbd.shtml)

Someone in a good position to wonder has a bad feeling about it ...

> Daniel Radcliffe, who plays Harry Potter in the movie versions of the books, admitted on the set of the forthcoming Goblet of Fire film that he fears Voldemort can only be killed if the boy wizard dies too. (Toronto Sun, 9/5/04).

Whether Harry will ever graduate from Hogwarts.

> But when she was asked if Harry would ever get to wear Hogwarts graduation robes, she said: 'It would give quite a lot away if I answered that, so I am not going to.' (Scottish Daily, 7/9/04)

Things we will not find out until book seven

The final revelation:

josh from Cottenham Village College: Right at the beginning, when Voldemort tried to kill Harry, how did Voldemort and Harry both survive? *Schools Competition Winner*

JK Rowling replies -> That is the crucial and central question and if I answered it there would be hardly any point writing books six and seven... so I won't! ✗

Book Eight and beyond

There will not be an eighth Harry Potter novel

J. K. Rowling has said a lot of different things about her plans after she finishes book seven. She has wavered a bit on occasion

> Several people have asked "Are you stopping at seven?".
>
> J.K. Rowling:
>
> Um, at the moment I, I, I definitely think I'm going to stop at seven, and as I say, that will be really heartbreaking. Um, the only reason you'll ever see an eighth Harry Potter book is if I really, in ten years time, burn to do another one, but at the moment I think that's unlikely. But I try never to say 'never anything', because at the moment if I say 'I will never', I do it next month! So I just, I, but I think not. I just think we're gonna stop at seven (NPR, 10/20/99)..

More recently, she has been consistent in saying that book seven will be the end of the Harry Potter story, and that it will feel complete and final.

> "I think it highly unlikely I'll write more novels. I've got enough for seven books and I never meant to carry the story beyond the end of book seven," she said. (AP, August 5, 2004).

Fortunately, there are other possibilities! Read on to learn more. ✗

There may be a revised edition of the entire series

In a World Book Day chat in April 2004, Rowling appeared pretty interested in doing a revised edition of the series—let's call it Harry Potter version 1.1.

> Tanya J Potter: If you could change anything about Harry Potter what would it be?
>
> JK Rowling replies -> There are loads of things I would change. I don't think any writer is ever completely happy with what they've written. One of these days - once seven is finished - I'll revise all seven books (World Book Day Chat, 3/04/04, http://www.mugglenet.com/jkrwbd.shtml).

Although this sounds pretty positive, my gut feeling is that she won't do this revision for a while. The reason is simple: it will be a lot of work for her, and not terribly interesting work at that. She's a creative person, and she will want to spend her time and energy on writing new stuff!

On the other hand, this talk of a revised version is great news for her publishers. Once she revises the series, they can sell seven *more* books to each of her fans. It is also great news for Harry Potter fandom, since it means there will be two versions of the "canon" to argue over, and any theory can always be supported by a reference to an alternate version of the story. ✗

We will not see "Harry Potter: Episode One"

George Lucas has made three very expensive and critically disliked "prequels" to his "Star Wars" series. J. K. Rowling does not want to follow in his footsteps.

> Will there be a book about Harry's Mum and Dad, about how they became friends and how they died?

> So it would be "Harry Potter: Episode One". [Laughter]. No, but a lot of people have asked that. It is all George Lucas's fault. You won't need a prequel; by the time I am finished, you will know enough. I think it would be shamelessly exploitative to do that. I am sure that Mr Lucas is doing it only for artistic reasons, but in my case I think that by the time you have had the seven books you will know everything you need to know for the story. (Edinburgh Book Festival, 8/15/04).

And confirmed on the website:

> Hmm... once again, too much Star Wars can do this to a person. No prequels are planned. (jkrowling.com, http://www.jkrowling.com/textonly/rumours_view.cfm?id=6) ⚡

Harry Potter book eight: an encyclopedia?

Although there won't be an eighth novel, there may very well be an eighth *book* in the Harry Potter series, according to J. K. Rowling.

> She said: "I'm not going to say I'll never write anything to do with the world of Hogwarts ever again. Because I have often thought that (if I wrote) book eight, I think it would be right and proper that it should be a book whose royalties go to charity entirely."
>
> "It could be the encyclopaedia of the world (of Hogwarts) and then I could rid myself of every last lurking details, but no not a novel." (Ananova, 12/01, http://www.quick-quote-quill.org/articles/2001/1201-ananova-staff.htm)

The Encylopedia would be similar to her two previous charity books, "Fantastic Beasts and Where to Find Them" and "Quidditch Through the Ages" – but probably much longer!

The Encyclopedia will certainly include lots of good stuff on the students at Hogwarts.

> She has [a]booklet of every pupil. Their parentage in terms of allegiances to dark forces. Their magical ability. Every character is there in alphabetical order. (J. K. Rowling, Harry Potter and Me Special, 12/28/01, http://www.mugglenet.com/jkrshow.shtml)
> Troels Forchhammer shows a screenshot of this page at
> http://www.hogwarts-library.net/reference/HarrysYear.html

There will be more about dementors, but not 150 pages worth.

> Kirk Wilkins: Will you ever publish all your notebooks of information on the series? I am very interested in reading 150 pages on the history of the dementors!
>
> JK Rowling replies -> lol! Who said there were 150 pages on the dementors??? I certainly didn't! I don't think I'll ever publish my notebooks. Too many revealing doodlings! (World Book Day chat, 3/04/04, http://www.mugglenet.com/jkrwbd.shtml)

It's interesting that she is perfectly willing to talk about publishing an encyclopedia, but not her notebooks. What could she be hiding? Ok, it could be just personal stuff … "I heart Harry" … but maybe there's more to it than that! Some tantalizing details about Harry Potter may have to wait until Rowling's death, or beyond.

J. K. Rowling used "Fantastic Beasts" and "Quidditch" to bury some potentially important facts, like the fact that Hermione's companion, Crookshanks, is not just an ordinary cat. Watch for the Harry Potter encyclopedia to include a few buried nuggets that cast a new light on the events of the series. Also expect Rowling to use the encyclopedia to correct persistent misunderstandings of her work—for example, don't expect the entry on "Draco Malfoy" to make him sound like a good boy to marry! ✗

What else can we expect from J. K. Rowling??

We can expect J. K. Rowling to keep writing creatively! It seems to be something that she needs to do. She's already dreading the end of the series.

> I'll just keep writing. I'll probably just start a completely new plot in book seven. It's going to be very difficult to leave it. I mean, I do look forward to a post-Harry era in my life, because some of the things that go along with this are not that much fun, but at the same time, I dread leaving Harry... because I've been working on it over what I sincerely hope will prove to have been the most turbulent part of my life and that was the constant, and I worked on it so hard for so long - then it will be over and I think it's going to leave a massive gap. (BBC, 6/19/03; http://news.bbc.co.uk/1/hi/entertainment/arts/3004456.stm)

That's a tantalizing hint there about "starting a new plot" in the middle of book seven. Is it possible that she will return to the world of Muggles and witches, but without Harry Potter? The answer to that may depend on the outcome of book seven.

It sounds as if she is still feeling creative.

> JP: Do you know what you will go on to next after that?
>
> JKR: Well, while I was in between, during the three years I've just had [between GoF and OOtP], I was writing something else for a while which was really great, it was good, and I might go back to that. I don't know.
>
> JP: Is that an adult novel?
>
> JKR: Mmmm. It's just something completely different. It was very liberating to do it. (CBBC Newsround, 6/19/03, http://news.bbc.co.uk/cbbcnews/hi/uk/newsid_3004000/3004878.stm).

The problem she faces is that her second act will be under incredible scrutiny.

> JP: Be quite difficult for you though. You'd have to publish under a pseudonym wouldn't you?
>
> JKR: Exactly. But they'll find out within seconds. I don't underestimate the investigative powers of the press, but I don't know what I'll do. (CBBC Newsround, 6/19/03, http://news.bbc.co.uk/cbbcnews/hi/uk/newsid_3004000/3004878.stm).

Expect her to write, and to be published.

> I mean, I know I will definitely still be writing. Will I publish? I don't know. It's what you said, of course you

write to be published, because you write to share the story.
(CBBC Newsround, 6/19/03,
http://news.bbc.co.uk/cbbcnews/hi/uk/newsid_3004000/3004878.
stm).

Just be ready for some whining by critics and even by fans.

But I do think back to what happened to AA Milne, and he
of course tried to write adult novels, and was never
reviewed without the mention of Tigger, Pooh and Piglet. And
I would imagine that the same will happen with me. And
that's fine. God knows my shoulders are broad enough, I
could cope with that. (CBBC Newsround, 6/19/03,
http://news.bbc.co.uk/cbbcnews/hi/uk/newsid_3004000/3004878.
stm).

And for a possibly maddening delay!

… I would like some time to have some normal life at the
end of the series, and probably the best way to get that
isn't to publish immediately. (CBBC Newsround, 6/19/03,
http://news.bbc.co.uk/cbbcnews/hi/uk/newsid_3004000/3004878.
stm).

Last but not least, we can expect J. K. Rowling to continue as a strong
advocate for good in the world. The Sunday Times (South Africa) reported this
great item in late summer 2004:

"After reading a recent report that six mentally
handicapped children had been discovered in cages in a
Prague mental institution, Rowling wrote a fearsome letter
to the Czech ambassador in the UK, saying she was "horrified
beyond words. The very idea of being locked in a cage around
the clock is enough to give adults nightmares."

Just a day after it had been handed to that country's
president, he ordered the removal of caged beds for both
adults and children in all psychiatric facilities. It's not
only on Earth, then, that JK Rowling is storing up her
riches." (Sunday Times [South Africa], 8/23/2004). [Well
said!—wfz] ✗

Appendix A

Differences between US and UK editions of *Harry Potter and the Half-Blood Prince*

Source: http://www.designit-digital.com/hp6.htm

Harry Potter and the Half-Blood Prince			
US Page	US [ISBN 0-439-78454-9]	UK [ISBN 0-7475-8108-8]	UK Page
2	fewer than ten	less than ten	7
2	how dare anyone	how dared anyone	8
2	moved over to the window	moved over to the windows	8
3	small, dirty oil painting	small and dirty oil-painting	9
4	forward	forwards	9
4	toward	towards	10
5	how he felt	how he had felt	11
5	Minister of Magic	Minister for Magic	11
6	throw me out the window	throw me out of the window	11
8	Prime Minister rather resented	Prime Minister had rather resented	13
8	and drew up a chair	and drawn up a chair	14
8	Fudge pulled out his wand	Fudge had pulled out his wand	14
8	talked for more than an hour	talked for over an hour	14
9	Minister could shout	Minister had been able to shout	15
13	grand effect," he said. "The office	grand effect. The Office	18
14	they are," he said. "Killed in a room	they are. Killed in a room	19
15	around	round	21
18	A team of healers [...] are examining	A team of healers [...] is examining	23
18	he had a toothache	he had toothache	23
20	woman named Narcissa	woman called Narcissa	26
21	street named Spinner's End	street called Spinner's End	27
22	as though it was not usually inhabited	as though it were not usually inhabited	28

25	Sorcerer's Stone	Philosopher's Stone	31
32	Snape had gotten to his feet	Snape had got to his feet	37
34	as though it was encased	as though it were encased	29
42	4. Agree on security questions	4. Agree security questions	45
42	use of the Polyjuice Potion	use of Polyjuice Potion	45
44	as though the sudden darkness were an	as though the sudden darkness was an	47
46	your agapanthus	your agapanthuses	48
48	scared looks at one another	scared looks at each other	51
51	shag carpet	shagpile carpet	54
56	in other words, at the moment he	in other words, the moment he	57
57	conversation with the headmaster	conversation with his headmaster	59
57	not to mention done his best	not to mention doing his best	59
57	outside of Hogwarts	outside Hogwarts	59
65	furniture flew back to its original places	furniture flew back to its original place	66
66	Hmpf	Humph	67
66	so short they did not	so short that they did not	68
69	Dumbledore strode from the room	Dumbledore crossed the room	70
69	then crossed to the fire	then strode to the fire	70
73	Harry zip up his jacket	Harry zipping up his jacket	74
73	watched Dumbledore fasten his	watched Dumbledore fastening his	74
75	spider, spinning a web around it	spider, spinning a web around him	75
79	onward	onwards	80
81	nervous voice he recognized	nervous voice that he recognized	81
85	everybody's in mortal danger	everybody's in mortal peril	85
88	something hard inside the pillowcase	something hard in the pillow-case [Note: hyphen in "pillow-case" at line break]	88
92	avoiding one another's gaze	avoiding each other's gaze	91
97	sunlight streaming into his lap	sunlight streaming on to his lap	96
98	gazed at one another	gazed at each other	96
99	part of last night's conversation	part of the previous night's conversation	98

103	'Exceeds Expectations' at Defence	"Exceeds Expectations" in Defence	101
103	"Outstanding" at Defence	'Outstanding' in Defence	101
103	top at Defence	top in Defence	101
104	heard the prophecy a few weeks ago	heard the prophecy a month ago	102
112	Madam Malkin, the owner, said	Madam Malkin said	109
115	farther	further	112
115	Ron's and Harry's new robes	Ron and Harry's new robes	112
117	around the head and neck, and boxes of	around the head and neck; boxes of	114
117	pairs of briefs	pairs of pants	114
118	through the back	through to the back	115
119	black horn-type objects	black hooter-type objects	116
120	"Do they work?" she asked.	'Do they work?'	117
122	put it back then	put it all back then	118
124	under the cloak nowadays	under it nowadays	120
127	Mr. Borgin squinted at her	Borgin squinted at her	123
127	said Mr. Borgin coldly	said Borgin coldly	123
131	slip in it." Harry smiled.	slip in it,' smiled Harry.	126
132	zat Tonks," Fleur mused, examining	zat Tonks,' mused Fleur, examining	126
133	if he was to tell anyone	if he were to tell anyone	128
133	Mr. Weasley was the right person	Mr Weasley would be the right person	128
133	the prefects' carriage	the prefect carriage	128
136	lost to view	lost from view	130
137	*Quibbler* still going	*The Quibbler* still going	131
139	beamed Luna. Then she pushed	beamed Luna, and she pushed	133
142	as though he was expecting	as though he were expecting	135
142	great silvery mustache	great silver moustache	136
143	greeting, nor did Harry	greeting, and nor did Harry	137
143	wiry-haired youth	wire-haired youth	137
145	as though he was a particularly	as though he were a particularly	139
147	Slughorn said, sounding	Slughorn continued, sounding	140
149	upward	upwards	142

153	His eyes lingered for a moment upon Harry's trainers. xxxx"You didn't hear	His eyes lingered for a moment upon Harry's trainers. 'That was you blocking the door when Zabini came back in, I suppose?' xxxxHe considered Harry for a moment. xxxx'You didn't hear	146-147
156	on Harry to Crabbe, Goyle, Zabini, and Pansy Parkinson.	on Harry to his fellow Slytherins	149
156	where he could be recounting his attack	where he would be recounting his attack	149
157	and they began a	and the train began	149
157	corridor. She pulled open	corridor. Tonks pulled open	149
157	momentum. He followed her	momentum. Harry followed her	149
160	backward	backwards	152
162	swung open into the vast	swung open on to the vast	154
167	mention of his name; he merely raised	mention of his name, merely raised	159
168	your own and other's safety	your own and each other's safety	160
171	miniscule first-year boy as they joined	miniscule first-year as they joined	163
172	ducked under her arm	ducked under Hermione's arm	164
173	class schedules	timetables	165
174	Hmph	Humph	165
174	schedule	timetable	166
175	apart from a half dozen seventh years	apart from half a dozen seventh-years	167
176	from the fourth-year student. It zoomed	from the fourth-year. It zoomed	167
178	again, the class watched him	again, the class watched him	169
180	the Beaters on last year's	the Beaters on the previous year's	172
183	who grinned back lazily	who grinned lazily back	174
186	made a "shhing" gesture	made a 'shush'ing gesture	177
188	There was silence	There was a silence	178
196	"Acid Pops," said Harry, and the gargoyle	'Acid Pops,' said Harry. The gargoyle	185

196	to do with him this evening	to do with him that evening	186
219	see the marks on the back of your hand where that evil	see the marks where that evil	207
224	The second group was comprised of ten	The second group comprised ten	211
225	broad-chested third-year boy who had	broad-chested third-year who had	212
226	grinned at the team	grinned around at the team	214
228	flowery apron	flowery pinny	215
229	schedules	timetables	216
230	spider, Aragog, who dwelled	spider, Aragog, that dwelled	217
230	suckers and stingers	suckers and stings	217
231	when we were there last summer	when we were there in the summer	218
232	*was* Confunded this morning. And he was	*was* Confunded. And he was	219
240	bed again!" Ron grinned, helping	bed again!' grinned Ron, helping	225
243	furry hat and an overcoat	furry hat and overcoat	229
244	display of Cockroach Clusters.	display of Cockroach Cluster.	229
246	who was slowly turning purple	who was turning slowly purple	231
246	She watched them go through the door	She watched them through the door	232
248	as though she was about to fly	as though she were about to fly	234
250	trying to quiet her	trying to quieten her	235
261	mass of memory from when he had come	mass of memory whence he had come	245
265	drained her own glass in one gulp.	drained her own glass in one.	249
268	She looked around at Dumbledore again	She looked at Dumbledore again	251
272	possessions must be in there	possessions must have been in there	255
281	Meanwhile, Ron, who was	Ron, meanwhile, who was	263
282	try hooking up with McLaggen	try getting off with McLaggen	263
282	hit the bowl and shattered it	hit the bowl and it shattered	264
282	*I hooked up with McLaggen*	*I got off with McLaggen*	264
282	sitting here with the pair	sitting there with the pair	264
286	kissing fiercely as though glued	kissing fiercely as if glued	268

289	elder-brotherly	older-brotherly	271
293	drained it in one gulp	drained it in one	274
294	Harry smiled back vaguely	Harry smiled vaguely back	275
299	said Harry, grinning broadly	said Harry, now grinning broadly	279
301	just as the portrait hole was closing	just in time to see the portrait hole closing	281
301	look like he would be surfacing soon	look like surfacing soon	281
304	Charms next morning	Charms the following morning	285
308	book that's been written on!	book that's been written in!	288
310	greater than Ron's just now	greater than Ron's just then	290
314	a certain amount of giggles from	a certain amount of giggling from	294
314	set of [...] robes that were attracting	set of [...] robes that was attracting	294
315	was a small, stout, bespectacled man	was a small, bespectacled man	295
319	first lesson, Draught of Living Death	first lesson, The Draught of Living Death	299
320	what I'd like to do," said Harry defiantly.	what I'd like to be,' said Harry defiantly.	299
320	working to bring down the Ministry of Magic from within using	working from within to bring down the Ministry of Magic using	299
322	room ... Harry pressed his ear	room ... but Harry pressed his ear	301
324	reliance in assistants	reliance on assistants	303
327	Fred, who had turned it into a paper airplane	Fred, who turned it into a paper aeroplane	306
327	sprout knife at	sprouts knife at	306
330	large wooden wireless set.	large wooden wireless.	309
339	package that came	package which came	317
342	checked her name	checked on her name	320
343	garden, and Percy	garden and then Percy	321
344	at him so he pretended	at him, so pretended	322
344	out of the corner of his eye	out of the corner of his eyes	322
346	to check that people really are	to check people really are	325
354	before the 31st August next	before 31st August	331
354	they had a great deal of nerve	they had a great nerve asking	331

	asking		
355	as though he was a gorilla	as though he were a gorilla	332
355	object of today's Charms lesson	object of that day's Charms lesson	333
356	Dumbledore's hands lay on either side of it	Dumbledore's hands lay either side of it	333
368	did memories go bad?	did memories go off?	345
369	Harry recognized Voldemort at once.	Harry recognized Riddle at once.	346
369	retiring?" he asked.	retiring?' Riddle asked.	346
370	Voldemort, however, stayed behind.	Riddle, however, stayed behind.	347
371	except that Voldemort had asked	except that Riddle had asked	347
371	see Slughorn or Voldemort at all	see Slughorn or Riddle at all	347
376	He glanced around at Ron	He glanced at Ron	352
378	"You've got nerve, boy!"	'You've got a nerve, boy!'	354
379	memory. Well? Hasn't he?"	memory,' said Slughorn. 'Well? Hasn't he?'	356
382	Apparition Tests in this time	Apparition test in this time	358
382	Heads of Houses	Heads of House	358
384	face the front again.	face the front.	360
385	concentrate continuously upon	concentrate continually upon	361
385	lost balance	lost his balance	361
386	back to the Gryffindor Tower	back to Gryffindor Tower	362
391	impractical idea; Harry had lessons	impractical idea; he had lessons	366
400	recounted, it felt like	recounted what felt like	375
404	brain like his," said Hagrid.	brain like his,' said Hagrid staunchly.	379
406	Heads o' Houses	Heads o' House	380
406	Hagrid's and Filch's raised voices	Hagrid and Filch's raised voices	381
407	not pleased to be woken	not pleased to be awoken	381
408	the Potions master's	the Potion master's	383
409	and that now that Harry was	and that now Harry was	383
412	changing rooms	changing room	386
414	dirty-blonde hair, nor the necklace	dirty-blonde hair, or the necklace	387

417	only just arrive on time for the match	only just arrived in time for the match	391
420	continued to try and kick	continued to try to kick	393
423	corridor that was deserted	corridor which was deserted	396
423	turned onto a seventh-floor	turned into a seventh-floor	396
426	up to this point	up to that point	398
427	my staffing problems	my staff problems	400
431	from him," he said earnestly.	from him,' Harry said earnestly	402
431	the Award for Special Services to	the Special Award for Services to	403
434	flourishing potted plants	flourishing pot plants	406
437	scarlet at the words	scarlet at her words	409
437	was back in its red velvet cushion	was back on its red velvet cushion	409
442	and who have twice, I think	and who has twice, I think	414
442	why you—who are so often asked	why you – who is so often asked	414
448	the only other people awake were	the only other people still up were	419
449	Fred and George's Spell-Check ones	Fred and George's Spell-Checking ones	421
450	ink all over his freshly completed essay	ink all over his essay	422
459	in the paper about	in the *Prophet* about	430
459	open your books to page	open your books at page	430
459	organizing their things	organising its things	430
461	seemed to merely irritate	seemed merely to irritate	432
463	Harry pulled the Marauder's Map	Harry pulled out the Marauder's Map	434
463	wished Ron and Hermione both luck	wished Ron and Hermione luck	434
470	narrow, slanted writing	narrow, slanting writing	440
474	smugness, excitement, or superiority	smugness, or excitement, or superiority	444
475	wonderful," said Slughorn an hour and a half later, clapping his hands together as	wonderful,' said Slughorn clapping his hands together an hour and a half later, as	444
476	not twenty-four hours' worth	not twelve hours' worth	445
477	smiting, brimming with confidence	smiling, brimful of confidence	446

480	there were acromantulas in the forest	there were Acromantula in the Forest	449
481	but if there was any way	but if there were any way	450
481	the beast only just died	the beast has only just died	450
482	face-to-face with the acromantulas	face to face with the Acromantula	451
482	stopped them from eating Hagrid	stopped them eating Hagrid	451
483	said Hagrid in a shaking voice	said Hagrid in a shaky voice	452
483	through the trees now, and its rays	through the trees and its rays	452
486	Pekingese	Pekinese	454
488	xxxx*And Odo the hero, they bore him back home* xxxx*To the place that he'd known as a lad,* xxxxxxxxsang Slughorn plaintively. xxxx*They laid him to rest with his hat inside out*	Slughorn sang plaintively: xxxx'*And Odo the hero, they bore him back home* xxxx *To the place that he'd known as a lad,* xxxx*They laid him to rest with his hat inside out*	456
490	Harry leaned	Harry leant	458
494	much younger Slughorn	much younger Horace Slughorn	462
494	the half-dozen teenage boys	the half a dozen teenage boys	462
502	maintain their immortality	maintain his immortality	469
502	transformation he has undergone	transformation he had undergone	469
504	as you now know, for many years I have made it my business to	as you now know, I have made it my business for many years to	471
504	But would Lord Voldemort use	But Lord Voldemort use	471
504	what I have showed you	what I have shown you	471
508	discredit Arthur and get rid of a highly incriminating magical object in one stroke	discredit Arthur, have me thrown out of Hogwarts and get rid of a highly incriminating object in one stroke	475
508	if he is not secretly glad	if he is secretly glad	475
509	his magical powers remain	his magical power remain	475
511	Harry, but then, he was in	Harry, but he was in	479
520	known his team to fly better	known his team fly better	486
521	he was unable	he was often unable	487
521	inside the Room of Requirement, he	inside the Room, he	487

521	He could not hear anything.	He couldn't hear anything.	488
521	lest Filch turn up	lest Filch should turn up	488
522	Harry slipped as Malfoy	Harry slipped over as Malfoy	488
526	large cupboard that seemed	large cupboard which seemed	492
527	gazing around at all the clutter	gazing around at the clutter	493
527	he stood it on top of the cupboard	he stood it on the cupboard	493
530-531	however, little though he knew he deserved	however, though he knew he little deserved	496
534	triumph, he grinned down	triumph, Harry grinned down	499
536	forced to study for hours	forced to revise for hours	501
539	*A Thousand Magical Herbs and Fungi*	*One Thousand Magical Herbs and Fungi*	503
544	in my room.	in my room at the inn.	508
548	as though he was fighting	as though he were fighting	512
551	"I've got to be quick," Harry panted	'I haven't got much time,' Harry panted	515
551	"What does he want?"	"What does Dumbledore want?"	515
551	fetch your Invisibility Cloak	fetch your Cloak	515
552	into Hermione's hands	into Hermione's hand	515
553	through the portrait hole and toward	through the portrait hole towards	516
555	cliff stood behind them, a sheer drop	cliff stood behind, a sheer drop	519
556	niches made footholds leading down	niches that made footholds led down to	520
558	he now pointed his wand	he pointed his wand	522
561	suggestion. But he was much keener	suggestion, but much keener	524
565	as though an invisible rope was pulling it	as though an invisible rope were pulling it	528
567	given Ron and Hermione Felix Felicis	given Ron and Hermione the Felix Felicis	530
569	not want to *immediately* kill	not want *immediately* to kill	532
571	as though he was deeply asleep	as though he were deeply asleep	534
571	three goblesful of the potion	three gobletfuls of the potion	534

573	glass; then Harry was	glass; Harry was	536
575	struggling to cling to the smooth	struggling to cling on to the smooth	538
577	extreme pallor and by his air of exhaustion	extreme pallor and his air of exhaustion	540
582	flying behind him on the night air	flying behind him in the night air	544
583	broom shudder when	broom shudder for a moment when	544
583	so they could enter at speed	so that they could enter at speed	544
584	who gestured him to retreat	who gestured to him to retreat	545
585	some of your guards.	some of your guard.	546
587	... there is a pair I take it?" xxxx"In Borgin and Burkes," said Malfoy	... there is a pair, I take it?' xxxx'The other's in Borgin and Burkes,' said Malfoy	548
591-592	"He cannot kill you if you are already dead. Come over to the right side, Draco, and we can hide you more completely than you can possibly imagine. What is more, I can send members of the Order to your mother tonight to hide her likewise. Nobody would be surprised that you had died in your attempt to kill me—forgive me, but Lord Voldemort probably expects it. Nor would the Death Eaters be surprised that we had captured and killed your mother—it is what they would do themselves, after all. Your father is safe at the moment in Azkaban. . . . When the time comes we can protect him too. Come over to the right side, Draco . . . you are not a killer. . . ."	'Come over to the right side, Draco, and we can hid you more completely than you can possibly imagine. What is more, I can send members of the Order to your mother tonight to hide her likewise. Your father is safe at the moment in Azkaban ... when the time comes we can protect him too ... come over to the right side, Draco ... you are not a killer ...'	552-553
591	he was suddenly white as Dumbledore	he was suddenly as white as Dumbledore	552
593	"That's right," said Fenrir Greyback	'That's right,' said Greyback	554
593	Greyback grinned, showing pointed	Fenrir Greyback grinned, showing pointed	554
593	He was not looking at Fenrir; he	He was not looking at Greyback; he	554

595	"I'll do it," snarled Fenrir, moving	'I'll do it,' snarled Greyback, moving	555
598	Harry felt Fenrir collapse	Harry felt Greyback collapse	558
598	him. It was the werewolf, Fenrir.	him; it was the werewolf, Greyback.	558
598	one of the fighters detached themselves	one of the fighters detached themself	558
599	right behind her. He launched	right behind her. Harry launched	559
600	bloody footprint that showed	bloody footprint which showed	559
600	brother and sister running	brother and sister Death Eaters running	560
600	he leapt the wreckage	he leapt over the wreckage	560
600	suit of armor that exploded	suit of armour which exploded	560
602	revealed suddenly behind clouds	revealed suddenly from behind clouds	561
603	somewhere overhead Snape was	somewhere above him Snape was	563
608	last half hour	last half an hour	567
608	beside him. He had known	beside him. xxxxHarry had known	568
609	force with which it hit the ground	force with which it had hit the ground	568
612	"Neville and Professor Flitwick are both hurt, but Madam Pomfrey says they'll be all right.	'Neville's in the hospital wing, but Madam Pomfrey thinks he'll make a full recovery, and Professor Flitwick was knocked out, but he's all right, just a bit shaky. He insisted on going off to look after the Ravenclaws.	571
612	a Killing Curse that huge blond one	a Killing Curse the huge blond one	571
616	sorry that they were dead." xxxxThey all stared at him. xxxx"And Dumbledore believed that?"	sorry that they were dead.' xxxx'And Dumbledore believed that?'	574-575
616	She looked disoriented	She looked disorientated	575
619	Ron had taken the map	Ron had taken the Marauder's Map	577
619-620	said Harry, who was watching Snape running up the marble staircase in his mind's eye,	said Harry, who in his mind's eye was watching Snape running up the marble staircase,	578

620	afterward	afterwards	578
620	up the stairs ... then	up the stairs to the Tower ... then	578
622	might be like when he awakens. . . ."	might be like when he wakes up ...'	580
623	Ron looked as stunned as he felt	Ron looked as stunned as Harry felt	581
629	governors, who will make the final decision	governors, who will take the final decision	586
630	"It is really true?	'Is it really true?	588
633	Entrance Hall that was resolved	Entrance Hall which was resolved	590
634	what he knew was right to do	what he knew it was right to do	591
637	looking out the window	looking out of the window	594
639	laid to rest. He had never	laid to rest. Harry had never	595
639	real to him once it was over	real to him once the funeral was over	595
641	Leaky Cauldron in London	Leaky Cauldron	597
641	recognize, but a few he did, including	recognize, but there were a few that he did, including	597
641	insubstantially on the gleaming air	insubstantially in the gleaming air	598
642	Fudge walked past toward	Fudge walked past them towards	598
642	Neville and Luna alone of the D.A. had	They alone of all the DA had	598
642	The staff was seated at last	The staff were seated at last	598
643	into both Ginny's and Hermione's laps	into both Ginny and Hermione's laps	599
646	as though the sunlight were blinding them	as though the sunlight was blinding them	602
648	favorite pupil ever.	favourite ever pupil.	604

Colophon

This book was produced using Microsoft Word and Adobe Acrobat. The cover was produced using The Gimp 2.0.2 with Ghostscript. The cover font is Palatino Linotype. The spine is Verdana.

Heading fonts and the body text inside the book are in Palatino Linotype, chosen because it is a nimble-looking font. Quotations are in Verdana, chosen because it has strong connotations of the Web and the Internet. The end of major sections is signified by the dingbat ⚡ from the Webdings font, chosen because it resembles Harry Potter's lightning bolt scar.

The American Heritage® Dictionary of the English Language, Fourth Edition, copyright © 2000 by Houghton Mifflin Company defines col·o·phon as follows:

> An ancient Greek city of Asia Minor northwest of Ephesus. It was famous for its cavalry.

Along the same lines, Webster's Revised Unabridged, copyright 1996, 1998, MICRA, Inc.:

> \Col"o*phon\ (k[o^]l"[-o]*f[o^]n), n. [L. colophon finishing stroke, Gr. kolofw`n; cf. L. culmen top, collis hill. Cf. Holm.] An inscription, monogram, or cipher, containing the place and date of publication, printer's name, etc., formerly placed on the last page of a book.

J. K. Rowling revealed something about *her* finishing stroke in a 1999 interview with People Magazine.

> "I constantly rewrite," [Rowling] says. "At the moment, the last word is 'scar.'" ⚡

Printed in the United States
70360LV00004B/124